THE EXPRESS

INVESTMENT
GUIDE

The Express Guides

The Express and Kogan Page have joined forces to publish a series of practical guides offering no-nonsense advice on a wide range of financial, legal and business topics.

Whether you want to manage your money better, make more money, get a new business idea off the ground – and make sure it's legal – there's an Express Guide for you.

Titles published so far are:

Great Ideas for Making Money
Niki Chesworth

Your Money
How to Make the Most of it
Niki Chesworth

Buying a Property Abroad
Niki Chesworth

You and the Law
A Simple Guide to All Your Legal Problems
Susan Singleton

How to Cut Your Tax Bill Without Breaking the Law
(Second Edition)
Grant Thornton, Chartered Accountants

Be Your Own Boss
How to Set Up a Successful Small Business
David McMullan

Readymade Business Letters That Get Results
Jim Douglas

The Woman's Guide to Finance (Second Edition)
Tony Levene

Buying Your First Franchise
G R Clarke

Your Home Office (Revised Second Edition)
Peter Chatterton

Available from all good bookshops, or to obtain further information please contact the publishers at the address below:

Kogan Page Ltd
120 Pentonville Rd
LONDON N1 9JN
Tel: 0171-278 0433   Fax: 0171-837 6348

Many thanks to everyone who assisted both in the preparation of this book in particular, and to all those who have offered me their help and expertise on investment matters over the past two decades. They are, of course, too numerous to mention.

THE ⛨EXPRESS

INVESTMENT GUIDE

Practical Advice for Making the Right Choice

SECOND EDITION

TONY LEVENE

**KOGAN
PAGE**

The author has no connection with any products or services advertised in this book. He takes no responsibility for their content and cannot advise on their merits or demerits.

First published in 1995
Second edition published in 1997

Kogan Page Limited
120 Pentonville Road
London N1 9JN

© Tony Levene, 1997

British Library Cataloguing in Publication Data

A CIP record for this book is available from the British Library.

ISBN 0 7494 2015 4

Typeset by Saxon Graphics Ltd, Derby
Printed and bound in Great Britain by Clays Ltd, St Ives plc

Contents

Introduction

Once the stockmarket was the preserve of the very rich. You had to have knowledge, expertise, a good stockbroker and above all money, the reasoning went, before you went anywhere near stocks and shares. And even then you treated the market with caution; even if you were not there, you did not forget the crash in the 1920s with stockbrokers hurtling from the top of very tall buildings – you have seen it at the cinema.

However, that perception is changing. The flood of privatisation issues in the 1980s introduced many ordinary households to the delights and secrets of the stockmarket, and share ownership is on the increase. According to the London Stock Exchange, the number of individual shareholders in the UK rose from 3 million in 1980 to 11 million in 1991. And in 1997, with the conversion of leading building societies into companies, that figure will jump to around 15 million – more than one in three of the adult population.

There are even more of us who are affected by the stockmarket. It is the basis of almost all our investments — not just the obvious ones like unit trusts, but also pensions, endowment policies and much else.

Even so, stocks and shares can be risky investments; they are not as safe as putting your money into the building society. For every investor who made millions out of putting money into the likes of The Body Shop, there are those who came a cropper by staking their shirt on Polly Peck or British & Commonwealth — and unlike most other areas of financial services, there is no compensation scheme to call on when you realise that the men in whom you have invested your financial security have had their hands in the till for years.

Nevertheless, stocks and shares can add to your financial wellbeing if handled correctly. Continuous and cautious investment might not make you a millionaire, but it can add to your security in old age and provide a sound back-up to the major financial decisions you make in your life.

Alternatively, if you do not wish to invest directly in the stockmarket, there are any number of ways to spread the risk: investing through unit or investment trusts, for example. This book aims to lead you through the stockmarket maze: assessing what your financial needs are, how much risk you are prepared to take, finding a stockbroker and other ways of investing in the stockmarket.

We will also look at rights issues and how to deal with them, dividend payouts, having fun with stocks and shares, and there is a section dealing with your tax position.

So do not be afraid, the stockmarket is no longer just the preserve of the rich. Use it carefully, use it wisely and use it well — and who knows? Even if you do not end up joining the ranks of the super wealthy yourself, you should, at least, be better off.

Phone Sharelink for the Best Introduction to Stocks and Shares – 0121–200–2242.

Look after the pennies and the commission could look after itself

CATERDEAL

SHAREDEALING

Private investors regularly trading in shares are always looking for a bargain. When they use CaterDeal Direct, that's what they get. The ability to conclude their deals during one phone call. And at share prices which are guaranteed to be the *best* available – sometimes even better! A share price improvement of just half a penny can often more than cover CaterDeal's low commission charges. It could even be more.

CaterDeal Direct commission charges from just £9 per trade. Annual membership £21.15. Free (optional) nominee service. Order lines open 7 days a week from 8am to 9pm weekdays, 9am to 5pm Saturdays, 10am to 4pm Sundays.

Cater Allen Sharedealing High Interest Cheque Account, cheque guarantee card, gold credit card also available. No bank charges.

If you're looking for a real bargain, call us now.

CALL ☎ 01708 74 22 88

Or return the coupon, FREE, to CaterDeal Sharedealing Service, Freepost, Romford, Essex RM1 4BR

✂

Please write in

TITLE; MR/MRS/MS/OTHER		PERMANENT ADDRESS
FIRST NAMES (IN FULL)		
SURNAME		
DAYTIME TEL No.		POST CODE

CATERDEAL

IG/3

HOW TO KEEP YOUR INVESTMENTS ON TRACK

There are two main risks when investing:

① Your investment will not keep pace with inflation.

② Your investment may fall in value.

Christine Ross from Abbey National Independent Financial Advisers Limited puts these points into context with one of the most important investments you may ever make.

Investment is usually associated with lump sums. Whilst investment can be used to provide capital growth, income, or a combination of both, one of the largest investments anybody makes is for their pension. This might be through an occupational pension scheme which can be supplemented, if necessary, with an additional voluntary contribution (AVC) or free standing additional voluntary contribution (FSAVC). If a company scheme is not available then a personal pension plan will normally be used.

Circumstances or preference may also lead to investment for retirement through other vehicles, such as deposit accounts, Tessas, PEPs, unit trusts and endowment policies.

The level of saving is often dictated by what is affordable, and this can be the most important consideration. However, if you are saving with a particular goal in mind – for example, a certain percentage of your salary as pension in retirement, it is important to establish your target, and then save towards it. Of course it is not possile to predict the precise level of investment return in the future, nor will you know how your earnings will increase or what inflation will be.

Even though this type of planning cannot be a precise science, using sensible assumptions, we can help you work towards your target income in retirement.

One of our consultants would carry out an initial consultation with you which would involve just answering a series of very simple questions about you and your family, and any financial details. This information would be input onto our Lifeplan system, annd working with the consultant, would help to identify your priorities. The system is interactive so that you may set a target, and using those assumptions, the system would calculate the amount of regular contributions, then the consultant would reduce the contribution level to what you could afford, and the system would then calculate the final projected fund at the target date. You could then have this contribution level reviewed next time you meet with your consultant.

Once the general goals have been set and agreed, the consultant would then prepare a report covering the recommendations to you to enable you to achieve your financial plan.

The key benefits of Lifeplan are that it is an interactive system that provides a method of targeting your savings and investments to meet your goals. It can help target any shortfalls, and is particularly important with pension planning where the achievement of these goals will determine whether or not you have enough income to enjoy your retirement.

Regular reviews of your financial plan are just as important as the establishment of such a plan. It is essential that you make sure that you remain on track to achieve your ojectives.

If you would like to arrange an appointment for a financial review please call free on 0800 18144 quoting reference DE1.

ABBEY NATIONAL
INDEPENDENT FINANCIAL ADVISERS LIMITED

Regulated by the Personal Investment Authority

A lasting and living memorial to your generosity

The English countryside has been the delight of countless generations – yet this very heart of our national heritage is constantly under threat from damaging development.

Working at national and local level since 1926, CPRE has played a major part in the creation and protection of National Parks, the provision of Green Belts around cities and in establishing firm planning controls. Important contributions are also being made to agricultural, forestry, water and transport policies and hedgerow protection. CPRE's success is based on solid research, constructive ideas and reasoned argument.

CPRE is ever-vigilant but its work as a small but cost-effective charity is totally dependent on public support. By making a bequest or a donation to CPRE, you can help to ensure that England's Green and Pleasant Land is enjoyed by future generations. Remember, a legacy to a registered charity like CPRE is exempt from Inheritance Tax.

REGISTERED CHARITY NUMBER 233179

If you would like further information about remembering CPRE in a will, write to David Conder, Room 14, Council for the Protection of Rural England, Warwick House, 25 Buckingham Palace Road London SW1W 0PP

PATRON HM THE QUEEN
PRESIDENT JONATHAN DIMBLEBY

CPRE

*Your countryside
Your voice*

1

Your Investment Objectives

'May you live in interesting times', runs the old Chinese curse, and it has certainly been an interesting time in the financial services industry over the last few years. Scandal after scandal has thrown a shadow during the last few years over the investment community from Robert Maxwell's pilfering of his companies' pension funds to the more recent outrage when it emerged that figures from a leading unit trust, managed by Morgan Grenfell, owed more to the manipulative skills of its manager than to his ability to pick winners.

So who can you really trust nowadays? How can you build up your savings and investments without having the lot swiped by a modern-day highwayman who steals with the use of calculators and computers, technology and jargon, rather than simply by holding a pistol to your head?

With caution and knowledge, is the answer. The more you know about financial services and the stockmarket, the more you will be able to be on your guard when it comes to looking after — and building up — your own money. You can do a lot of the building up by yourself — you do not always need a whole host of financial advisors charging the earth for the privilege of telling you what to do with your own money.

Before you start thinking about investment though, there are a number of other financial necessities that you have to cater for. First and foremost, you should have a lump sum in the building society stowed away for a rainy day. You should not even think of putting money into the stockmarket before you have the necessary readies to tide you over in case of emer-

gency. Some people say that this should be the equivalent of a year's salary; and although that is highly unrealistic for most of us, you should try and have at least the equivalent of three months' earnings squirrelled away.

Next, you should also make sure that you have adequate pensions provision. You should join your company's scheme if you are able to. If you do not qualify, then you should take out a personal pension plan. You can pay up to 17.5 per cent of your salary into a personal pension plan up to the age of 35, after which the maximum allowed payments go up in stages. If you are in a company scheme, you could also take out additional voluntary contributions, as long as combined with the company scheme, overall payments do not exceed 15 per cent of your salary. You should also make sure that your mortgage or the amount at which you rent a property is adequately catered for, and that you are covered by the appropriate insurances. Only then is it time to start thinking about investment.

Almost anyone can build up an investment portfolio, no matter how small the sums you have to put aside. Just £20 a month is enough to set you on the path of greater wealth, if you invest it wisely.

The first thing to do when you set out to build up a portfolio is to decide how much money you can afford to set aside each month. Be reasonable about this. It is tempting to think that you will be able to put hundreds aside without feeling the pinch, but before you decide to do this work out exactly what your other financial obligations are and how much you can realistically afford to invest. It is better to do this than to set up a savings plan only to have to dismantle it a couple of months later when you realise you cannot keep the payments up. That could actually entail losing money. Your investments could have fallen, and you may face charges for selling them.

Next you must decide what you are investing for. Do you want to build up your capital, or are you investing for an income? How long-term are your savings plans? If you are building up capital, do you want it to provide financial security on retirement, or are you simply saving up for a new car or even a particularly special holiday?

On the whole, investment is an activity for the longer term. If you are saving up for a holiday next year, it would probably be better to put the money into a high paying account in the building society. If you are thinking of taking the plunge into stockmarket waters, you should have at least a five-year timescale, and preferably one longer than that.

Age will be a factor when you are making your investment decisions. If you are nearing retirement or already receiving a pension, it is likely that the investments you make should be geared towards producing a long-term income. If, on the other hand, you are much younger, you should be investing with a view to building up capital — which you can reinvest to provide an income when you are older.

Then there is the risk factor — how much money can you afford to lose? Stockmarket investment always involves risk. One rule is to spread your exposure to potential calamity as widely as you can. The size and rating of a company is no guarantee that catastrophe will not strike. A few years ago, Asil Nadir's Polly Peck was the darling of the investment community and a member of the prestigious FT-SE 100, an index of Britain's leading companies. Then it went bust and Nadir himself fled the UK in a light plane to go, out of reach of UK justice, to North Cyprus.

Even though it is extremely unlikely that a blue-chip company like British Telecom or Glaxo-Wellcome would ever hit the skids in the same kind of way, remember that all-important maxim: investments can go down as well as up. There is no guarantee, however distinguished the company, that its share price will not fall. This can happen either quickly if some unforeseen calamity occurs, or slowly if, say, a competitor gradually begins to build up market share. (Although if this does happen, you should remember that even if the share price falls, you should still receive an income from dividend payouts.) There are ways of spreading the risk, such as investing in unit or investment trusts, which we will look at later, but there is no guarantee that you will come away with as much money as you put in.

2
All About Shares

Before you can decide how to make the stockmarket make money for you, you should take a look at how it works. There are currently around 2,000 companies listed on the Stock Exchange with a further 200 or so on the Alternative Investment Market, a low regulation home for small and new companies. These quoted concerns range in value from many billions to under £1 million.

These companies all have a finite number of shares (also known as stocks or equities) that can be bought and sold. When you buy a share, you are buying a stake in the company, and that stake entitles you to an income in the form of dividends as well as a number of rights and opportunities.

Share prices

You can find out the price of a share by looking at daily listings in newspapers such as *The Express*. These listings will be broken down into sectors depending on the company's business: Banks, Electricity, and Leisure and Hotels, for example. The total number of shares in issue multiplied by the share price will tell you how much a company is worth. Share prices are always quoted in pence, not pounds, up to £10: if a share is worth £3.20 it will be referred to as 320p.

The share price that you see listed in the newspaper will be the middle market price, and will not be the actual price at which you buy or sell. There are two prices quoted on the stock market 'screens'. When you buy a share, you buy it through a stockbroker at the offer price, that is, the price at which the stockbroker is offering to sell the share. When you sell, you sell it through the stockbroker at the bid price, the level at which the stockbroker is bidding to buy the share. The bid price is always lower than the offer price, and the difference between the two is known as the spread. This means that, in effect, as soon as you buy a share you lose money, as you will not be able to sell it again immediately at the same price. The price must move enough to cover the spread before you start to make a profit.

The spread is often a good way of judging a share's liquidity. Liquidity is the term used to signify how easy it is to buy and sell the shares of one company. If the spread of one company's shares is much wider than the average, that could mean that the market in that company's shares is not very liquid — it also means that you could have a problem if you wanted to sell the shares. You may have to accept a lower price – especially if you wish to sell many shares.

Stockbrokers have a duty to provide best execution — that is, to get the best price for you available in the market at that moment in time.

As share prices can move so rapidly, it might not always be possible for your broker to tell you the exact price at which he is able to buy or sell, especially in 'illiquid' shares. Prices are equally likely to move for or against you. But if you have a limit either for buying or selling, tell the broker. You might also want to give your broker several hours leeway to find the best price available — although this can be risky as the market may move against you. If you do this, always set a limit on the price at which you are prepared to deal.

The share price is affected by any number of factors. These could take up hundreds of volumes. But everything relies on the basic law of supply and demand. If buyers outnumber sellers, the price rises. And if the opposite applies, the value of the share drops.

Many people, however, want more concrete reasoning. If analysts in the City who follow the company think that profits are going to go up, the share price may move up accordingly, and if profits are due to go down the share price may slip. Confusingly, share prices sometimes fall after a company has announced good results. This is because the price will have risen in expectation of the result — it has been 'factored in' to the price — and when the figure is finally out, holders of the shares sell to take profits. This is known as profit taking, and fits in with an old stockmarket saw: 'Buy on the rumour, sell on the announcement'.

Analysts will also be looking at the years ahead. A company might have announced good results this year, but it might operate in an area where the long-term prospects do not look so good, in which case the City will be cautious about the shares. In these cases you will usually be able to tell by reading the press what the longer term view of a company's prospects are.

Share prices are also affected by external factors. For example, in the case of some utility stocks such as the water companies, the share prices will be affected by price limits set by Ofwat, the industry regulator. Equally, British Telecom's price was affected when rival Mercury was allowed a bigger participation in the market. Share prices will also respond when a takeover bid is launched. When Company A bids for Company B, the latter's share price almost always shoots up. Stockbrokers know that Company A will want to get hold of most of Company B's shares — as long as the price does not rise too high. If the City thinks that the takeover will also be advantageous for Company A, perhaps by giving it a greater share in its market, Company A's share price will also rise.

External economic factors will also influence share prices. If there is a rumour going round that interest rates are about to rise, share prices will generally be marked down. This is because higher interest rates mean that it will be more expensive for a company to fund itself by borrowing on the market. It also means that the general economic climate will be more difficult, thus making it harder for the company to sell its products and make profits. The deposit rates at banks and building societies will inevitably rise, and thus become an attractive alternative to stockmarket investment.

If a company is going to make an announcement that will affect the price of its shares, for example, by saying that it is going to launch a takeover bid, it will usually notify the Stock Exchange in advance. The Exchange will then usually suspend the share price until the announcement has been made to ensure that no one will be able to profit from the information until it is made known to the public.

There are also some less scientific theories about what moves share prices. There is an old stockmarket adage: 'Sell in May and go away and if you want to make it pay, come back on St Leger Day' (the second Saturday in September). Historically, there has been some truth in this. In the eighteenth century, farmers had to borrow money from the City in the spring to pay their workers over the summer. This forced interest rates up and equities down. Then in the autumn, flush with cash after the harvest, they would lend money back to the City with the opposite effect.

After that, the rich were to blame: they would sell their shares to pay for Royal Ascot, the Season and and a long summer retreat. Then they would return in time for the St Leger, win on the horses and invest in the market (in theory, anyway). And there is the 'January' effect. Share price rises are often strongest in the first days of the year. Sell in May is doubtful, but buy in January has been a winner – provided you were well prepared and made your purchases along with sharper investors in December! Remember that you will have to pay commission for every transaction, which might outweigh any gains you make, as well as stamp duty on purchases. The gains, if any, are liable to be thin.

Stockmarket indices

It is not enough simply to know what the price of one share is doing, you have to look at the market as a whole. Share price movements across the market are averaged out and measured in a series of indices and they are also divided into sectors, such as oil companies or insurers, so that you know how a share has performed against its direct competitors, as well as the market.

The most commonly used index is the FT-SE 100. It is simply an index of the UK's 100 largest companies, and it is usually the index referred to on the radio or television when you hear that the market has gone up or down.

This has largely supplanted the FT 30-Share Index, also known as the Financial Times Ordinary Share Index, which charts the movement of 30 (not necessarily the largest 30) major companies. There is also the FT-Actuaries All-Share Index, known as the All-Share, which covers the top 800 companies as well as the sector indices, and ones that measure smaller and medium-sized companies. On top of that, there are indices for foreign stockmarkets.

All of these indices, listed in the back pages of the *Financial Times*, will give the previous day's price movement, the high and low for the year and other information that you need when judging a share such as the average dividend yield (see below) for the shares in the index.

Share prices go up and down with the market in general; they also have their own characteristics. A share that goes up 20 per cent when the market rises 10 per cent has done well, but the same share price gain when the market as a whole has risen 30 per cent is far less impressive.

Dividends

Shareholders usually receive dividends: a certain amount of income paid out per share every year. Dividends are paid out of the company's profits. However, they are not guaranteed — dividend payouts can be cut as well as raised — and if a company has performed very badly, it might not pay out a dividend at all. Dividend payouts are usually made twice a year; these payouts are known as the interim dividend and the final dividend. When they are paid out, tax has been deducted at 20 per cent; we will go into more detail about that when we look at tax later in the book.

You can usually opt to have the dividend payouts sent to you by cheque or paid directly into the cheque account of your choice.

Dividends have been the subject of some controversy recently. Some analysts believe that pressure on companies from institutional investors, such as pension funds and insurance companies, to pay out ever-increasing dividends has harmed businesses in the long-term. It is thought that the money should have been ploughed back into research and development. But others say it is better to hand money to shareholders who can make decisions on what to do with the money rather than entrust directors who might 'spend it for spending's sake'!

Dividend cover

One way of assessing whether dividend payouts will remain stable or fall is to look at a company's dividend cover. At its simplest, dividend cover is the number of times that net profits, or 'earnings' will cover the dividend payouts. The figure is reached by dividing the profit by the payouts. For example, if a company made net profits of £100,000 and paid out £25,000 in dividends, the dividend would be covered four times.

If dividend cover falls from one year to the next, or ceases to exist at all, it could be a sign that the company is in trouble. In order to stay popular with the institutions during the recession, some companies paid dividends out of reserves, the equivalent to the money they held in the bank.

Dividend yield

This is one of the ways in which the stockmarket rates your shares, and it gives you an idea of what other people think about your investment choice. A high yielding share in comparison with similar companies or the market in general might provide you with a better return, but it might also mean that the market expects profits to fall and has marked the share price down accordingly. Alternatively, a low yield may mean that profits are expected to rise and the share price has been marked up.

Don't forget that the yield is not the same as the dividend in pence per share. If the shares pay out a dividend of 10p, you are not necessarily getting a return of 10 per cent because the share price is unlikely to be 100p. The actual return is worked out through the dividend yield, which takes into account the income received as a percentage of the money you paid for the share. The formula is this: divide the gross dividend per share by the share price and multiply by 100. Confusingly, the dividend yield does not take into account the 20 per cent tax automatically deducted from dividend payouts.

Total return

Stockmarket professionals add the dividends to any share price movement to obtain the 'total return'. Tax considerations apart, a 10p dividend each year for five years is worth more than a 49p increase in the price of a share paying no dividend.

Scrip dividends

Some companies offer shareholders scrip dividends. That means that your dividend is paid to you in shares rather than cash. If you are offered the alternative of taking either, it is often worth taking the shares rather than the money as this is a cheap and easy way of adding to your shareholding. You pay no stockbroker's commission. However, non-taxpayers cannot reclaim the tax deduction.

3
Setting Up Your Portfolio

When setting up your portfolio, you must first decide what you want to achieve — for example, income or capital growth — and then choose how to achieve it. Income seekers should aim for companies with prospects of rising dividends and enough capital growth in the share price to keep up with inflation. Growth seekers aim at long-term share prices and can ignore dividends. On this will depend what kind of sector you are going to invest in, and the individual shares you choose.

How much have you got?

This will determine not only the number of shares but the sort of investment. A small-to-medium sized portfolio (between £10,000 to £50,000) should have a quarter of its money in gilts, a quarter in overseas funds (ideally through unit trusts or investment trusts) and the rest in UK equities. Stockbrokers say that all investments in the portfolio should be for the longer term. And it is very important that you do not throw your profits away in dealing costs. In other words, resist the temptation to buy and sell too often as any profits might be eaten up in stockbrokers' commission.

Now you have to decide which sectors of the stockmarket to invest in. Smaller investors should minimize risks, which means investing in blue-chip stocks. Blue-chips are the aristocracy of the stockmarket: big, safe and well-known companies like Marks & Spencer and British Telecom. The only trouble with these companies is that while they are unlikely to fall in value, unless they are following the market down in which case they should eventually recover along with the index, neither are they desperately exciting in the short-term. However, blue-chip shares can be particularly good for a long-term income, rather than short-term capital growth.

That is the next choice you must make: whether you want your shares to provide income or capital growth. If you want to secure an income, look for high-yielding shares. Remember that there is sometimes a reason for the high yield — that the market does not consider them a safe bet. The major exceptions to this rule are utilities stocks such as gas, water and electricity. These companies are considered to be very safe, but they provide a high yield because of their very strong cash flow — all of us, including very large companies, have to pay our gas bills regularly. Equally, these shares are unlikely to provide strong capital growth because there will not be massively increased demand for, say, electricity next year, and the individual companies cannot increase their market share at the expense of a competitor. But there is always the chance of a boost from a takeover bid. There is a one-way balancing act between yield and growth – one comes at the expense of the other. You cannot have high dividends and above-average capital growth – at least not for long. But you can have low dividends and no capital growth – or worse.

Capital growth is more likely to come from other stocks which are in fashion. Spotting the trend can be profitable. Oil was once profitable – and who knows, the privatised railways might recover their mid-Victorian pre-eminence. Pharmaceutical companies used to be popular growth shares because when a new drug was launched, it would provoke a dramatic increase in the share price. Now, the pharmaceutical glory days have gone. Enormous competition in the market has forced drug prices down and the companies are no longer the stockmarket stars they used to be.

This brings us to another area of the stockmarket: cyclical stocks. So-called because these are companies whose fortunes move in line with the economic cycle, they can make a lot of money for you if you invest at the right time — and lose a great

EXPLODING THE MYTH

"Stockbrokers only deal for the very rich". Wrong! Around ten million people already own shares and many more know something about the stockmarket through the Government's privatisation programme.

Stockbrokers are far removed from the stereotyped images often portrayed in the popular press and above all are approachable, friendly and accessible. You would probably be surprised to learn that about 95% of the population lives within 10 miles of a stockbroker's office.

Almost all of the firms who look after individual investors in shares are members of the Association of Private Client Investment Managers and Stockbrokers (APCIMS), the trade association which promotes those firms and, by extension, the interests of the private investors who use their services.

What makes APCIMS members different?

Direct Access to the Market - the majority of our firms are members of the London Stock Exchange and are therefore unique in having direct and immediate access to the stock market for buying and selling shares. The computerised systems used mean that brokers do not have to be located in the City of London - they can be in your local high street.

Professionalism - the breadth and depth of investment experience and knowledge which APCIMS members make available to their clients contrasts with that of many other financial advisers whose expertise is limited to the selling of a handful of "packaged" products offered by the big insurance companies.

Genuine Independence - APCIMS members are truly independent unlike other financial advisers many of whom are "tied" to a particular company. The advice given by our members is completely impartial and their charges are disclosed to you in advance.

Tight Regulation - all APCIMS members are regulated by either the Securities and Futures Authority (SFA) or the Investment Managers' Regulatory Organisation (IMRO). They are subject to demanding tests of their financial resources and are obliged to meet the most rigorous procedural standards and management controls. Only those individuals who are personally registered with the regulators as being "fit and proper" are authorised to give investment advice.

Individually Tailored Services - APCIMS members operate on the basis of providing services which are tailored to suit your individual circumstances and requirements.

The main services available are:

Advisory Services - almost all APCIMS members offer an advisory service in which the professional advises on the purchase, sale or retention of individual stocks.

Dealing or "Execution-Only" Service - this service is designed for investors who do not require advice but who do need a stockbroker to buy and sell shares for them.

Discretionary Investment Management Service - to put it simply, this service gives the manager the authority to buy and sell investments for you without obtaining your prior approval on each and every occasion.

Comprehensive Financial Planning - this can include advice on the placing of cash deposits, pensions, mortgages, life assurance, Personal Equity Plans (PEPs), Tax Exempt Special Savings Accounts (TESSAs) and so on.

How To Find Out More

A comprehensive brochure and a directory of APCIMS members detailing the range of services they offer are available free of charge by writing to APCIMS at 112 Middlesex Street, London E1 7HY, quoting reference DE97.

FTSE 100

Stock	Price (p)	Market value £ billion	Stock	Price (p)	Market value £ billion
3i	480.5	2.83	Mercury Asset Mgt	1222.5	2.23
Abbey National	706.5	9.94	Nat Power	450.0	5.45
Allied Domecq	419.5	4.35	National Grid	185.0	3.16
Argos	751.5	2.15	NatWest	663.0	11.32
Asda	121.8	3.57	Next	562.5	2.10
Assoc Brit Foods	463.0	4.17	Orange	181.0	2.17
BAA	481.5	5.00	P&O	578.5	3.52
BAe	1125.5	4.85	Pearson	694.0	3.96
Bank Scotland	292.0	3.49	Powergen	561.5	3.57
Barclays Bank	1002.5	15.45	Prudential Corp	471.5	9.06
Bass	812.5	7.17	Railtrack	357.0	1.78
BAT Inds	490.5	15.20	Rank Group	427.5	3.57
Blue Circle Inds	360.5	2.66	Reckitt & Colman	671.5	2.73
BOC Group	887.5	4.29	Redland	351.5	1.83
Boots	591.0	5.34	Reed Int	1034.5	5.88
BP	661.0	37.29	Rentokil	438.5	6.26
British Airways	576.5	5.77	Reuters	694.5	11.72
British Gas	231.0	10.18	RMC	961.5	2.49
British Steel	167.5	3.41	Rolls Royce	241.0	3.56
BSkyB	476.5	8.20	Royal & Sun Allnce	425.5	6.62
BT	390.5	24.80	Royal Bank	537.5	4.39
BTR	250.5	10.06	RTZ	933.5	10.00
Burmah Castrol	1044.5	2.20	S&N	655.0	4.04
Burton Group	152.5	2.21	Safeway	382.0	4.14
Cable & Wireless	452.0	10.11	Sainsbury (J)	354.0	6.50
Cadbury Schweppes	487.0	4.87	Schroders	1505.0	2.85
Carlton Comms	494.5	2.87	Scottish Power	336.0	3.90
Cookson	207.5	1.42	Severn Trent	652.5	2.40
CU	665.0	4.51	Shell Transport	985.5	32.67
Dixons	547.0	2.30	Siebe	987.5	4.67
EMI Group	1289.0	5.59	Smith & Nephew	177.5	1.97
Enterprise Oil	571.5	2.82	SmithklBchm	807.5	22.20
GEC	371.0	10.29	Smiths Ind	746.0	2.27
General Accident	688.0	3.32	Southern Electric	774.5	2.00
GKN	1041.5	3.68	Std Chartered	690.0	6.78
Glaxo Wellcome	942.5	33.41	Tate & Lyle	448.5	1.96
Granada	856.0	7.31	Tesco	345.0	7.48
Grand Met	433.0	9.10	Thames Water	570.0	2.14
GRE	261.0	2.37	TI Group	537.0	2.56
Guinness	434.5	8.39	Tomkins	245.0	2.92
GUS	628.5	6.32	Unilever	1342.5	10.94
Hanson	82.5	4.30	United News	646.5	3.17
Hays	537.5	2.23	United Utilities	575.5	3.02
HSBC	1232.5	32.30	Vodafone	247.0	7.56
ICI	777.0	5.63	Whitbread 'A'	775.0	3.77
Kingfisher	611.0	4.11	Williams Hldgs	346.0	2.01
Ladbroke	217.0	2.54	Wolseley	426.0	2.42
Land Securities	712.5	3.65	Zeneca	1607.5	15.22
Lasmo	216.0	2.09			
Legal & General	348.0	4.31			
Lloyds TSB	413.0	21.17			
Marks & Spencer	483.0	13.65	Source: Bloomberg Financial		

deal if you do not. Two examples of cyclical stocks are chemical and engineering companies, which do well when the economy is booming. Chemicals are manufactured in large plants and when the plants are full chemical companies can increase their profit margins; when they are half-empty, margins must be drastically cut back. Similarly, engineering plants are more likely to secure large orders when an economic upturn is on the way.

Building and construction companies are also cyclical stocks, but should be treated with caution until it is very obvious that the economy is booming again. Other sectors that depend on consumer spending are, for example, breweries, household goods, property, leisure and hotels.

Other shares that are of interest are financial shares, although the price of these tends to be dictated by interest rate movements, and media stocks. These have an element of risk but are popular with small investors who are familiar with the names of big television companies. Spirits, wines and cider are also popular shares with investors because they know more about the companies, but if you are interested in them you should be careful; most are dependent on world demand as well as that in the UK.

There is another category of shares that attracts some interest: penny stocks. Penny stocks are so-called because their price is only a few pence. These stocks tend to be highly speculative; if something happens to improve the company's fortunes they can rocket upwards by several hundred pence.

Equally, if a share with a 3p price rises 1p, it has gained a third. A 100p share rising the same amount only gives a 1 per cent gain. That is the theory. In practice, most penny shares remain in pennies, and because of 'illiquidity' the profits may be more apparent than real.

The 'buy' price of a share with a 3p mid price might be 3½p, and when you try to sell, you may just get 3½p rather than 4p – as the spread is ½p either side. Your 33⅓ per cent profit has now been wiped out – and that's before dealing costs and stamp duty.

However, remember that there is no guarantee that this will happen — and remember also that a company's share price should reflect the value of that company. A share can be cheap at 1000p and expensive at 2p.

Picking your share

One way for a private investor to build up a portfolio is through new issues which are often 'priced to go' – attractively low – and do not entail dealing costs but this is dependent on their frequency. Additionally, it is difficult for small investors to get a piece of the new-issue pie — the lion's share goes to the big investment institutions. So if you want to build up an active portfolio, you will have to do so by picking shares that are already available on the market.

There is no surefire way to pick a share that is going to become increasingly valuable and produce a handsome stream of dividends along the way; if there were, we would all be rich. Always keep clear of anyone offering a 'system' to beat the market. These are usually frauds. If anyone really knows how to make a stockmarket mint, why should they a) share it and b) waste their time in marketing? Nevertheless, there are a number of factors that you can take into account before buying a share.

The report and accounts ,

The report and accounts is one of the most important sources of information about a company. It is sent out once a year and includes a chairman's statement, talking about events over the last year, general information about the company's businesses and financial information that includes the previous year's profit or loss.

One theory has it that the size of the chairman's picture or the number of sightings of the corporate helicopter in the report is in direct proportion to the size of the fall of profits in the coming year. But there are more scientific pointers as well.

The profit and loss account

Stockbrokers recommend that you start by looking at the profit and loss account. The most important figure here is the pre-tax profits, but the profit and loss account contains more information that is crucial when you decide if you want to buy a share. Possibly the second most important figure is turnover. This shows how much business the company has actually done. If a company has a very high turnover, but has made only a small amount of pre-tax profit, it could mean that it has been forced to cut margins (ie the amount it sells a product for after manufacturing and labour costs have been taken into account) in order to keep the business going or it could simply mean that the business generates a lot of turnover. This could apply to businesses as disparate as a supermarket or a commodity trader. The trick is to compare with past years and with rival firms.

Underneath the turnover figure, you will find the costs the company has incurred throughout the year. These could include any number of items. Staff costs are one major expense. Another item you will often see is depreciation. This refers to how much the company's machinery and equipment has fallen in value over the previous year (although it is an accounting device more than a statement of fact).

When costs have been deducted from turnover, you arrive at the company's operating profit, also known as the trading profit. But there is one more item to take into account before you reach the pre-tax profit figure: interest. This can either be a plus or a minus figure, depending on whether the company has borrowed money and has to pay interest or has deposits and receives interest.

Now you have the pre-tax profit figure. Depending on the company, you either go straight after that to the tax bill or look at extraordinary items. So-called because they are one-offs, extraordinary items can again be positive or negative. For example, there can be a big loss because of widescale redundancies or a big gain because of the sale of part of the business. Don't be deceived by these, but they could provide clues to the company. Large-scale slimming down could be a pointer to further trouble ahead, or to the company making itself attractive to a bid, or indeed to a new start less the fat of the past.

The profits after tax will not all go to shareholders. It will be split in two or possibly three different ways. The company might have minority interests to be taken care of first. This happens when a company controls a subsidiary, but does not fully own it. The other shareholders in this subsidiary have the right to a certain amount of the profits — the size depends on their shareholding — of that subsidiary, even though the controlling company has included the full amount of those profits in its own operating profits. After that you get the amount paid out in dividends. Whatever is then left is called retained earnings, and is ploughed back into the business.

At the bottom of the account, you get the earnings per share (EPS) figure. The EPS is another important pointer as to whether you should buy a stake in that company because it shows how much profit the company is making per share in issue. To reach it, simply divide the net profit or earnings by the number of shares in issue. For example, if a company had made net profits of £100,000 and had 400,000 shares in issue, it would have earnings per share of 2.5p. Although this figure is not much use on its own, if you compare it to previous years, it gives some indication of whether the company is managing a steady increase in profits or just 'buying' in expansion at the expense of issuing more shares – the financial equivalent of spreading the jam more thinly.

You should also look at the notes at the end of the report and accounts. They will often contain much more detailed information than the profit and loss account, and it is here that you will find details of, for example, directors' contracts.

The balance sheet

The balance sheet is the other important page of the report and accounts; it shows the value of the company's assets (although not the value of the company — that is determined by the share price). The balance sheet starts by listing fixed assets. These are the solid, long-lasting assets: the company's factories, for example, the amount of land it owns and its machinery. On the other side, there will be loans from banks and other long-term debt. These will usually be broken down into categories.

Then there are the company's current assets, these are more ephemeral than the fixed assets. Current assets are cash in the bank, investments and amounts owing from other people or companies. Subtract current liabilities (the amounts the company itself owes) from current assets to arrive at the net current asset figure.

Fixed assets and net current assets are added to arrive at the total net assets figure. You then add shareholders' funds, this is the amount that belongs to the shareholders, but is not paid out in dividends. Shareholders' funds are made up of the retained earnings, which we saw on the profit and loss account, and of capital and reserves. The total amount will be the total worth of the company's assets. The key fact to remember is that the balance sheet is a once-a-year snapshot. By the time the report and accounts are published anything up to six months after the year-end, the position could have changed.

Net Asset Value per share

The Net Asset Value (NAV) of a company is another important indicator as to whether a business is doing well or not. At its simplest, it is what the shareholders would get back if the company were to be wound up, but it is complicated to work out. Not only must the company's assets be taken into account minus the liabilities, but you must also include elements that are difficult to quantify, such as goodwill.

Once you have worked out the NAV of the company, divide it by the number of shares in issue to work out the Net Asset Value Per Share. This will reveal the exact amount you personally will get back should the company be wound up. In most cases, the shares should be trading at a premium to the NAV. That means that the individual share price should be much higher than the net asset value per share, as the market expects the company to remain profitable well into the future. If the shares are very close to the NAV, or trading at a discount, warning bells should sound.

There are a few exceptions to this rule. For example, investment trusts and property companies where the assets are integral to the running of the business will often trade at a discount. Other companies could be trading at a discount simply because the market has undervalued them, in which case they could be prime targets for a takeover bid.

Other factors

You should also have a look at the chairman's statement for the previous year to see if it has any bearing on what the company went on to achieve. If the chairman forecast an unprecedented rise in profits along with winning five new contracts, whereas the company was actually forced to close down three factories and lay off half the work force, you might suspect that the current management was not best suited to run the company. You could also look at how many of the company's directors are also shareholders, and who the other major investors in the company are — anyone holding more than a one per cent stake in a company must declare it.

Stockmarket ratings

These will give you an indication of what the stockmarket thinks of your investment. One kind of stockmarket rating is the dividend yield, which we looked at in the last chapter. There are many others. The most commonly quoted is the price earnings ratio.

Price earnings ratio

The price earnings ratio, or p/e ratio, has nothing to do with how much income you will receive from your shareholding, but it is one of the most important pointers to whether you should invest in a particular company. Simply, it means how many years it would take for net profits (profits after tax, or earnings) to equal the current share price. The p/e ratio is worked out on the previous year's profits, and a high p/e ratio means that a company is expected to grow, whereas a low p/e ratio means that profits look set to fall.

The p/e ratio is worked out by dividing the earnings per share figure into the market price of the shares. In the example above, the EPS was 2.5p. If the market price of the shares was 60p, the p/e ratio would be 24, which means that it would take 24 years for the company's profits to equal the value of the shares.

This is actually a very high p/e ratio, which could mean one of two things: either the company has suffered a sharp fall in profits, or it is considered to be a growth stock. P/e ratios of over 18 are usually considered to be high, but you should not look at the p/e ratio of your chosen stock in isolation. You should compare it to the average p/e ratio in the sector you are looking at and compare that sector to the market as a whole. You will be able to find this information in the FT-Actuaries Indices at the back of the *Financial Times*.

Do-it-yourself analysis

There are any number of other considerations to bear in mind when picking a share. They can be highly personal. If you are considering buying shares in a chain of shops, wander by to see whether they are full. Examine the quality of the merchandise. Ask yourself whether it has a strong corporate image and how successful its own-label brands have been.

In addition of course, you should look at how economic news affects the company. Are strong competitors starting up in the same field? Is there any kind of government legislation coming in that will cause a problem for the company?

You should also look at the countries in which the company operates. Does it have businesses only in the relative tranquillity of Europe and North America? Alternatively, does it operate in volatile emerging economies or countries where businesses are likely to be nationalised?

Two increasingly important criteria that might affect your company are ethical investment and environmental investment. The two are slightly different. If you invest in companies on ethical criteria, you will generally want to avoid companies that involve armaments, tobacco and vivisection. Some geographical areas that have a bad record in human rights are also an ethical investment no-no. South Africa, for example, was once an absolute pariah as far as ethical investors were concerned, but since the ending of apartheid and the election of Nelson Mandela to the Presidency it has leapt into investment respectability.

Environmental investment is more proactive. Whereas ethical investment involves staying away from companies, environmental investment is based on actively seeking out companies that benefit the environment. Waste companies, and those involved in the clean-up of Eastern Europe are examples.

Listen to what people say about the company, and read the papers. Do you have friends who have bought the shares of a company and have been happy with their holding? Are the papers forecasting a takeover bid? Are there rumours about a change in management, and if so, why? Above all, will there be any problems about reselling your shares if you need your money back quickly? There are a number of other elements that you could consider such as shareholder perks, which we will be looking at later in the book.

4

Different Ways of Looking at Shares

More information is now produced on the stockmarket and the companies on it than ever before. But despite this flow of facts and opinions which are available to all investment professionals and to an increasing number of smaller investors through their stockbrokers, newspapers and the Internet, many fail to match 'stockmarket averages' such as the FT–SE 100 Index (the Footsie).

There are two entirely different options to the 'fundamental' method of looking through accounts and trying to figure out what market share a company may have and what the profit margins are likely to be over the foreseeable future. Both, in their different ways, say they can cut through the 'noise' produced by screeds of fundamental analysis.

The two are controversial, with many claiming they cannot work – or admitting they may work but they cannot figure out why. But both charting and picking shares with a pin – known to stockmarket theorists as the Random Walk method – have their strong proponents. The Random Walk has found greater acceptance in 'index tracking' or 'passive investments'.

Charts

Chartists claim they can forecast where a share price is going by analysing the pattern of its past price performance. Shares have their ups and downs, but they also have trends which suggest that the next movement will be in one direction or another. In

Share price – British Telecom

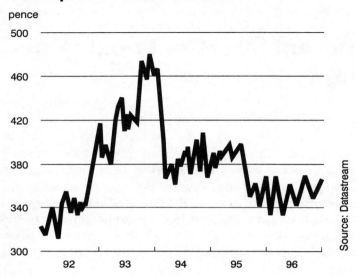

this, shares are no different from anything else in which supply and demand plays a role. A group produces a pop record. It takes time for fans to like it, but a chart will show that sales are building up. Once it has reached a certain level, huge numbers of people will want it – it will receive far more plays on the radio, for instance. Sales may stay at a high level for some time, but the signs of a falling off will become apparent.

Chartists, who often do not even know or care what the company does, say they can detect the same trends. They say that traditional analysts can use the same reason to explain why the market is falling as when it is rising.

The theory of charting takes up several large volumes, and making charts demands both a computer and a feed of share prices. The patterns can often be interpreted in more than one way, leading to disputes between chartists. Equally, there are several ways of drawing the patterns. Most are plain, such as the chart of the British Telecom share price. There are, however, 'point and figure' charts which record the major ups and downs in a series of noughts and crosses, and 'Japanese Candlestick' charts, with their 'spikes', 'real bodies', 'shadows' and even more esoteric and exotic labels.

The random walk and index tracking

If all this is too much for you, the best way of conquering the system is to let if flow with you. You can have as much success picking shares with a pin as at least half the unit trust managers in the UK, which sounds incredible. And when some bored journalists at the *Wall Street Journal* in New York decided to throw darts at their share price page in 1968, little did they dream that the portfolio they created would have beaten all bar one in twenty of the professionals over the subsequent years – but it has.

Why did that experiment – and many others since then in places ranging from Sunday newspapers to university research departments – work so well? Or even work at all?

Most of the price of a share contains all that is known about it, and there is little that is unknown about shares in major companies. So when something surprising happens which moves the share price up or down more than the average for the day, it is probably surprising to most people. The 'fundamental' researchers will have failed to discover it in advance – hence the surprise factor.

There is a limit, therefore, on how far you can forecast share prices by studying the company and all that surrounds it. Who can predict sudden price wars; or shortages; or revolutionary new inventions that make the company you invest in out-of-date overnight? Random Walk theory says that if you cannot forecast accurately, why bother?

When shares change hands, someone wins – perhaps they have sold a share which is about to collapse – and someone loses – the share they buy may go up but by less than the share they have sold. On that basis, you have a 50–50 chance of getting it right. But in reality, the odds are less than even, for, as we have seen, every transaction has a cost. Taking that into account, you have perhaps a 48 per cent chance of getting it right and a 52 per cent chance of making an error.

Every time that you trade shares, those costs chip away at the value of your portfolio. Buying a basket of shares – and the pin method does require that you spread your investment among 15 to 25 different stocks – and holding on to them not only saves time and worry. It also saves on transaction costs, and possibly having to pay for an investment manager. Add all the plus factors of the pin method together, and it is not hard to see that there is a strong argument for it. It is not one, however, that is often recommended in newspapers. It would, after all, deprive all those journalists who try to tip shares of a job! And it would also spell disaster for the publishers of tip sheets, one or two of whom have been in trouble with the Advertising Standards Authority for claiming a higher percentage of wins than they should have.

The pin method does demand a number of shares to ensure that you do not put all your eggs in one basket. This is known as 'diversification' and academic studies show that once you have 15–25 different shares in a portfolio, buying more does not spread your risks any further – rather, it just increases the costs involved. Stockbroking fees are geared to someone holding 10,000 shares in one company rather than ten shares in each of a thousand firms.

The Tracker Fund

What if you cannot afford to buy the required number of different holdings even though you believe that managers just cost money – they have to be fed and watered on a grand scale – and do not add value?

Many unit trust groups now have the answer. It is called the Tracker Fund or 'passive management'. It works on the 'as you can't beat them, you might as well join them' basis.

Instead of having a manager actively to research and choose shares, these funds employ a computer program which 'passively' buys every share in a given index – usually the FT-SE 100 in the right proportion. If companies are taken over, or the companies in the index change, the computer adjusts information so you always have a replica of the index.

When the index goes up 10 per cent, the fund rises by a tenth; if the index falls by 20 per cent, the fund falls by a fifth. There may be tiny percentages below or above the index due to various timing problems and whether the fund can buy at the exact share price used in calculating the index. This is known as 'tracking error' but as it can work either way, investors need not worry. There are many tracker funds for the UK, US and Japanese markets, with others due to come on stream as stock-markets around the world become more sophisticated. Because the computer does not demand an expenses account and a huge salary, these funds are cheaper to run than actively managed funds. Even a ½ per cent a year saving adds up to a tidy sum over five to ten years. The costs are kept down further by competition between unit trust groups for these funds.

But it is not just individual investors who put their money increasingly into tracker trusts. Huge pension funds often put tens of millions into similar funds because their combination of low costs and not losing money on wild bets means that, over time, they will always beat around two-thirds of rival active funds investing in the same market. And that is success.

Coming around a third of the way down the table does not qualify you as a record beater, but it is consistent. And managing to appear in the top half year after year has a cumulative effect. It is rather like the tortoise and the hare. Each year, there will be hares that will top the performance tables and boast about it in their advertisements. However, few funds or shares succeed in taking the pole positions two years running. Past performance is no guide at all to the future. You may be better off backing last year's loser than the winner over the previous 12 months.

The guaranteed fund

A variant of the index tracker is the fund which 'guarantees' to pay out the gain in a chosen index while promising that it will repay your original capital if the index selected is lower than the starting value when the limited life fund is repaid – usually in five to seven years. These sound attractive even though there are few instances of a major stockmarket being lower now than it was five to seven years ago. At the end of 1996, the Japanese stockmarket stood at little more than half its value at the end of 1989. This is the exception that proves the rule, but obviously no one knows when or where the next 'exception' will be.

There is a catch, however. These funds do not normally buy into the shares that make up the index but into 'derivatives' – Rocket Science devices such as futures and options – which can do many things, including substituting themselves for the real shares in the chosen index. And the creators of these derivatives want paying.

There is nothing for nothing in the stockmarket. So how is the apparent 'free lunch' of the guarantee paid for? The simple answer is that you forego the dividends on the shares when you invest in the market through futures and options.

Suppose you were in a six-year UK stockmarket fund. Giving up the dividends over that period would, after basic rate tax, be equal to losing around 15 per cent of your original capital. You invest £1,000 into a guaranteed fund. At the end of the time, the index rises by 1 per cent. The guarantee is not used. You get back £1,010.

Had you put the same capital in a Tracker Fund, you would have got back £1,010 plus dividends of around £150 – or more if you invested through a tax-free Personal Equity Plan. And you would have the flexibility to continue for longer or to have cashed in earlier according to your needs. These mathematics of 'guaranteed' funds do not appear in their prospectuses. But on the above dividend payment basis, your capital would have to drop below £850 – a fall of 15 per cent – before the guarantee starts to have any value. The next time that someone tries to sell you such a plan, ask how often the market has fallen by more than 15 per cent over the given period.

If you think there is a good chance of the market falling by that amount over the next five to seven years, you would be better off investing in a cash fund. Such pessimism is pointless in the stockmarket. And if you are more optimistic, what is the point of paying for the guarantee?

5

New Issues, Takeover Bids, Rights Issues and Scrip Issues

New issues

New issues are the life-blood of the stockmarket. If successful they bring in money for nearly everyone involved, they generate excitement, add liquidity to the market, and sometimes further the cause of wider share ownership.

Small investors have been particularly interested in new issues over the past 15 years because of the Government's privatisation programme. Privatisations are usually conducted on the same lines as a normal new issue, except that they are very much bigger, generate a huge amount of publicity and are aimed at small shareholders as well as 'institutions' such as pension funds and insurance companies.

Companies generally apply for a quote on the stockmarket when they want to raise money to plough back into the business, or when the founders wish to sell the business and reap the financial rewards for themselves. A company must have a trading record of three years when it applies to join the main market. The process is known as flotation, and when the company is actually quoted on the Exchange, it is also known as a listing.

New issues are one of the best ways for a small investor to build up a share portfolio. There is no commission payable to stockbrokers, and a successful new issue may start trading at a 'premium' — typically around 10 to 20 per cent above the issue price. This also provides the opportunity for short-term profit taking, known as 'stagging': when you stag an issue, you buy it with the specific intention of selling at a profit in the first few days of trading. In the past, speculative buyers have been known to borrow money to stag a new issue, but this does carry a risk: the issue might flop and the speculator will be left with no dealing profits with which to repay the bank. Professional 'stags' often used to put in multiple applications, a process now frowned upon, and, in some cases, illegal. That way, they ended up with lots of shares.

There are several types of new issue: an offer for sale, a placing, an intermediaries offer and an introduction. The last occurs when shares are already in existence and being traded, and the trading is being put on an official footing. No new money is raised, and introductions do not really involve private investors unless they are already shareholders.

An offer for sale is the normal way that private investors obtain shares in a new issue. A set number of shares is offered at a fixed price to the public at large. A placing occurs when shares are offered for sale privately to big institutional investors, although it is not uncommon for a new issue to be a combination of offer for sale and placing. An intermediaries offer occurs when shares are offered to intermediaries such as stockbrokers, who then make one application on behalf of all interested clients. If you apply through an intermediaries offer, you will normally have to pay commission.

When a new issue is about to be launched, it is underwritten by a broker, sometimes in partnership with a merchant bank. The broker (and the bank if it is involved) gets an underwriting fee, and guarantees to take up any shares that are left over after the issue has been launched. The broker then in turn places the shares with sub-underwriters, who also receive a fee, and also guarantee to take up leftover shares.

Brokers and institutions are usually very keen to get in on new issues: when the launch is successful, they will frequently want the shares themselves, and on top of that, they get their fees. One notable exception was the Government's £7.2 billion

	Launch date	Issue price	Current price	Gain from launch %	UK shares average
Amersham International	February 1982	142p	1040p	632	510%
Associated British Ports	February 1983	14p	274p	1857	374%
British Airports Authority	July 1987	122.5p	485.5p	296	69%
British Aerospace	February 1981	147.65p	1152p	680	559%
British Airways	February 1987	119.79p	594.5p	396	139%
British Energy	July 1996	203p	231p	14	6%
British Gas	December 1986	135p	232.5p	72	142%
British Steel	December 1988	125p	165.25p	32	113%
British Telecommunications	November 1984	130p	363.5p	180	249%
Cable & Wireless	November 1981	26p	483p	1625	553%
Enterprise Oil	June 1984	172.19p	548p	218	301%
Forth Ports	March 1992	101.28p	620p	512	65%
National Power	March 1991	175p	453p	159	63%
Northern Ireland Electricity	June 1993	220p	356.5p	62	37%
Powergen	March 1991	175p	577.5p	230	63%
Railtrack	May 1996	390p	511p	31	3%
Rolls-Royce	May 1987	165.66p	241p	45	103%
Scottish Hydro-Electric	June 1991	240p	305.5p	27	61%
Scottish Power	June 1991	240p	334.5p	39	61%
Water Companies	December 1989	222.27p	579p	164	67%
Electricity Companies	December 1990	225.31p	662.70p	196	86%

Source: Guinness Flight

Figure 5.1 How privatisation shares have fared

privatisation of British Petroleum in 1987. Just days before the launch was due, the stockmarket crashed, leaving the issue undersubscribed and the underwriters with millions of pounds worth of losses on their books. Such was the widespread anger at the losses (the Government could have postponed the issue) that the Bank of England was forced to step in and offer to buy back the shares at 70p.

In the run-up to a new issue, you will have the chance to assess whether the shares will be a good bet by following the financial press. This is where your knowledge of dividend yields and p/e ratios will play a part. Journalists will compare the new issue to companies already quoted on the Stock Exchange that operate a similar kind of business. Because the sponsor and the company concerned will want the issue to be a success, and will err on the side of caution, the company should be valued lower than its competitors. Check its historic p/e ratio and dividend yield against others in the sector (the information will be available, even though the company was not previously listed) and see how the new issue is rated against the others.

Shortly before the issue is due to be launched, there may be a 'pathfinder' prospectus if it is a big company. This gives most of the details except the final price. This will provide background information on the company. In many cases it is possible to register for a prospectus in advance. This is often worth doing if you are uncertain about investing in the company, as there is no obligation to buy the shares. And, of course, you will need to register in one way or another if you do intend buying.

With an offer for sale, you can apply for the shares either through an application form in the prospectus or through forms printed in the national press. If it is a popular issue, as almost all the privatisations were, the issue may be oversubscribed, in which case allocations – the amount of shares you end up with – will be scaled down. This means that you will get fewer shares than you applied for. Multiple applications —

when one person sends in more than one form applying for shares — are generally forbidden, but the privatisation issues allowed parents to apply for shares on behalf of their children as well as themselves. This boosts the total number of shareholders – artificially, some would argue.

As everyone concerned wants the issue to be a success, a company is usually slightly undervalued when it comes to the market. This means that when dealing begins, the shares sometimes trade at a premium to the issue price, giving a profit to anyone who wants to cash in straight away. The Government, in its desire to make the privatisation issues a success, became notorious for underpricing companies and providing small investors with an immediate profit. In the case of the first British Telecom issue in 1984, some investors literally doubled their money almost overnight, but later privatisations have been more realistically priced and have led to much smaller premiums. This is especially true of further sales of privatised company shares. Those who bought BTII made little, and those who purchased at the end of 1996 the more expensive BTIII were losing.

There is another way of pricing a new issue: through a tender offer where the shares are not offered at a fixed price. Investors are asked to state the number of shares they want and what price they will pay above a stated minimum. When all the applications have gone in, the sponsor will calculate the exact price at which the shares should be sold. This is known as the strike price and anyone who applied at that price or above has the chance to buy some of the available shares. However, tender offers are aimed at big institutions and are not usually suitable for the small investor, although the recent BSkyB flotation had many of the features of a tender offer.

Most new issues are fully paid; that is, you pay the full amount of the price up front. In some issues, most notably privatisations, investors are asked to pay in two or three instalments. That means that until the final instalment, you are holding partly paid shares.

The effect this has on the share price movement is known as gearing and can make you rich. For example, take a fully paid share of 100p, on which a first instalment of 20p has been paid. If the market thinks that the 100p share should trade at a 20 per cent premium, it will push the share price up to 120p. But the 20p partly paid share will also move up *by the 20 per cent premium on the 100p* — which means that it will double in value to 40p. The holder of the partly paid share thus makes a profit of 100 per cent as opposed to just 20 per cent. Partly paid shares are popular with speculators because of this exaggeration in the price movement. However, they are riskier than the fully paid version because if the share price falls, it will produce exactly the same effect in reverse and that will make you poor.

Some new issues, most notably the privatisations, have a loyalty bonus. This is to provide an incentive for investors to hold on to their shares, rather than selling them on for a quick profit. When British Gas was privatised in 1986, investors could opt either for one new share for every 10 held, up to a maximum of 500 bonus shares, or for £10 vouchers off their gas bills up to a maximum of £250. To qualify in both cases, investors had to hold on to their shares for at least three years. More recently, in the third tranche of the British Telecom privatisation, investors who held on to their shares for two years had the chance to opt either for an additional share bonus of one share for every 15 held, up to a maximum of 100 shares, or alternatively, 10p knocked off the price of the second and final instalments to a maximum of 1,000 shares.

Takeover bids

If you hold shares in a company that is the subject of a takeover bid, congratulations. You are almost certain to make some money. Takeover bids, like much else in the stockmarket, come and go in cycles; the early 1970s and late 1980s both saw frenetic periods of takeovers. Some suggest that bids indicate the top point for share prices. Others say the cash paid for the shares has a beneficial effect as it is reinvested in other shares.

Takeover bids are one of the best ways to make money in the stockmarket for almost everyone concerned: shareholders, lawyers, accountants, merchant banks and any number of other parties involved. You can read the financial press to try to gauge which company is likely to be the subject of a takeover bid and invest accordingly, but remember that any such buys would be highly speculative. You might not pick the right target, and even if you do, the bid might ultimately fail, leading to a drop in the company's share price.

When Company A launches a takeover bid for Company B, it can offer Company B's shareholders a number of options. It can pay for the shares in cash (which may incur a capital gains tax liability for the shareholder), it can offer to swap its own shares for those of Company B, or it can offer a combination of the two.

When a takeover bid is launched, you may be bombarded with literature from both sides — especially if it is a contested bid. It is usually worth hanging on for a while before you accept as the initial bid price is almost certain to be raised. The stakes are upped still further if a second bidder joins in the fun. Either way, when the final price is set, you should compare the value of the offer with the market price of the shares, and sell on the open market if you are set to make more there. But don't forget, you will incur costs.

A whole host of rules and regulations govern takeover bids, most of which do not concern the private investor. Nevertheless, it is worth knowing that when someone has bought a stake of one per cent or upwards in a company, they are bound to declare it, and when a company has built up a stake of 30 per cent or more it is bound to launch a takeover bid. The bid is conditional on a number of elements: the bid will usually lapse unless the bidder gets at least 50 per cent acceptances. If the bidder gets between 50 to 90 per cent of acceptances, he can either let it lapse or declare it unconditional, and if the bidder gets over 90 per cent acceptances, it will automatically become unconditional, and the bidder can acquire any remaining shares compulsorily.

Takeover bids are subject to something known as the 60-day rule. The bid must be completed within 60 days from the date that the formal offer documents are sent out; if not, the bid lapses and the bidder is not allowed at make a second attempt for another year. However, if a second bidder steps in, it will also be subject to the 60-day rule, in which case the second deadline also applies to the first bidder.

Once the bid has been made, there is one more potential pitfall: it might be referred to the Monopolies and Mergers Commission (MMC). This usually happens when the aggressor company threatens to get too large a market share in any one area. Bids often lapse after a referral to the MMC because the MMC usually takes about six months to report — too long to hold out for most companies. But what if you hold shares in the bidder rather than the target? The news can be less good. Stockmarkets hate uncertainty. No one knows if your company will get involved in a takeover battle leading to an 'auction'. Equally, investors will be unsure whether the bid is good or bad. Independent academic research shows that a takeover is positive for the bidder in 50 per cent of cases and negative in the other 50 per cent.

Rights issues

A company makes a rights issue when it needs more money and does not want to borrow from the bank. As the name implies, it gives existing investors the right to buy the new shares in proportion to the amount they already own. For example, a three-for-five rights issue gives shareholders the right to buy three new shares for every five they already hold.

The price will almost always be at a discount, typically 15 per cent lower than the price of the shares already on the market. If there is no discount, or the new shares are more expensive than those already in existence, do not go near them. Whatever the discount, the share price usually falls when a rights issue is announced because it dilutes the value of the shares already on the market. However, it does have some benefits for the small shareholder, it gives you the chance to buy more shares in the company without paying either stamp duty or the commission charged by stockbrokers.

If you do not wish to take up some or all of your rights to buy the new shares, you may still be able to make a profit by selling your nil-paid rights — the unused subscription price for the shares — through a stockbroker. If you do nothing at all and let your rights lapse, the company will usually sell your nil-paid rights for you and send you a cheque if there is any profit.

Scrip issues

Scrip issues, or bonus issues, are another way of increasing the number of shares you own in a company, but this time without paying a penny. A company will launch a scrip issue in the same language as a rights issue (three-for-five, which again means that you will get three new shares for every five existing), but you receive the shares automatically without paying for them.

However, this will not greatly affect the value of your holding. When a company launches a scrip issue, it is in fact really an accounting exercise that is creating the new shares out of the existing reserves, which is money that already belongs to the shareholders. The company's share price will adjust downwards to take account of the new shares, which means that the final value of your holding will remain roughly the same. But you could end up a little better. A scrip issue is often used when a share price is 'heavy' – over £10 – so you get more lower priced shares, which UK investors, unlike their American counterparts, are fond of.

Sharelink New Issues Services
0121–236–2126

6

Investing in Unit Trusts

If you are new to the stockmarket and worried about the risk of investing in a limited number of shares, or perhaps you are unable to buy enough shares to have a worthwhile holding, you should consider putting your money into a unit or investment trust. In broad brush terms, they are similar, but there are differences. We shall look at investment trusts in the next chapter.

Unit trusts will limit your exposure to risk by investing in a far greater number of companies than most individual investors could afford to do, and they are a good introduction to the pros and cons of share buying. They also cater to more adventurous tastes. As well as being able to invest in European companies through unit trusts far more cheaply and conveniently than if you bought the shares directly, you can even buy unit trusts based on developing markets in Eastern Europe, South America and Africa.

A unit trust is a fund that usually invests in the stockmarket, although some are 'cash' funds which concentrate on the money markets. It advertises its existence and hopes to take in millions from a large number of investors, which it then uses to buy the shares of a large range of companies. Unit trusts, along with investment trusts, are known as collective investments or pooled investments, because your money is being used to buy a range of instruments, using the money of many investors.

When you buy a unit trust, you are not buying the shares of any one of the underlying companies; rather you are getting a stake in the fund, the size of which is dictated by the number of units you buy. The value of the fund is dictated by the value of the underlying shares, which means that when the stockmarket falls, the value of a unit trust will also fall.

Unit trusts are known as open-ended funds, which means that the more money that is put into them, the bigger the fund is able to grow. A growing fund is often a sign of success. Conversely, if investors sell more of the units than they buy, the fund has to sell its underlying investments.

Unit trusts were born over 60 years ago, but it is only in the last 30 years that they have really caught on. They appealed to investors who wanted to invest in the equity market as they were fed up with low returns elsewhere. There are now about 1,500 unit trusts in existence, with an estimated 1.5 million investors holding around £125 billion worth of funds.

Ways to invest

If you decide to invest in a unit trust, you can either do so in a lump sum or through a monthly savings plan. The minimum investment in a lump sum can be as low as £500, even less in some cases, or from £20 a month. It is up to you which method you choose, but there are little appreciated advantages in using a monthly savings plan. If the market falls after you have made your initial investment, your next investment will buy more units. So you will have more should the price eventually rise – and that is obviously your goal. This is known as pound cost averaging. Equally, the opposite could happen. The shares could go up during the monthly plan and fall when you want to sell.

Some companies also offer share exchange schemes, which involve swapping shareholdings for units in a trust. They are ideal for small investors who might have a number of small shareholdings, gained through privatisation issues, for example, which they wish to cash in but do not wish to pay stock-brokers' commission in order to do so.

As with all investment decisions, you should decide whether to buy a unit trust to provide for you in the immediate future, the near future or the longer term. Ask the fund manager what the objectives of the fund are; that should tell you whether it is aiming for long-term capital growth or a short-term income.

If you think you might need to get your hands on your money quickly, you could consider a Cash or Money Market unit trust. Due to the amount of money invested, these funds are able to put your money — no matter how little — on deposit at a much better rate of return than most individuals could get at a bank. Some of these trusts even have a cheque book. However, they are not eligible to go into a Pep, a Personal Equity Plan whose tax-saving features appear in a later chapter.

If your savings horizons are one to five years, then there are two types of trust designed for this timescale: Bond unit trusts and Balanced unit trusts, also known as Managed or Mixed unit trusts. The former put your money into lower risk, lower return fixed-rate investments and the latter divide your money between fixed-rate investments and shares.

Bond funds are primarily designed to provide a decent level of income, which can be reinvested, as well as some capital growth. You can pick one that invests in UK government bonds, known as gilts, and UK corporate bonds, issued by companies. These are known as Gilt and Fixed Interest Funds. Alternatively, you can invest in International Bond Funds, which invest in fixed interest stocks issued all over the world.

UK Balanced Funds put your money into bonds and shares. Typically, they invest in shares that pay a high income, which means there is a real chance of both high income, and, possibly, capital growth to offset inflation. Again, the income can be reinvested. These funds can go down, and the bond element can easily be decimated if inflation takes off.

International balanced funds work the same way in the international markets, but are better for longer term savers as they carry the additional element of exchange rate risk. This works in

THE ☙ EXPRESS

NEW Titles from The Express series

Your Home Office
Third Edition
Peter Chatterton

If you plan to run a business from home or use a room there for occasional freelance work, you will need a copy of **Your Home Office.**

It describes how to choose and set up an office that will enable you to work efficiently, productively and profitably. Topics covered include:

◆ what basic equipment can provide the facilities of a modern office

◆ what it costs and how to make it pay for itself

£7.99 Paperback 0 7494 2234 3
160 pages March 1997

How to Cut Your Tax Bill
Without Breaking The Law
Third Edition
Grant Thornton

This jargon free guide unravels the complexities of the Inland Revenue and reveals ways for everyone to minimise their tax bill legally.

Bang up-to-date with new tax legislation **How to Cut Your Tax Bill** is the most succinct source of tax-saving tips available.

"a practical guide to all aspects of tax"

SUNDAY TIMES

"packed with information on how the tax system works"

GLOUCESTERSHIRE ECHO

£7.99 Paperback 0 7494 2016 2
176 pages March 1997

Available from all good book shops or to obtain further information please contact the publishers at the address below:

Kogan Page Ltd
Pentonville Road, London N1 9JN
Tel: 0171 278 0433, Fax: 0171 837 6348

THE★EXPRESS Guides:

Your Money

How to Make the Most of it (Second Edition)
Niki Chesworth

◆ a practical, reliable guide aimed at cutting through financial jargon
◆ invaluable advice on everything from banking and taxes to retirement
◆ essential to make your money work for you

£7.99 Paperback 0 7494 1641 6
128 pages 1995

Be Your Own Boss!

How to Set Up a Successful Small Business
David McMullan

◆ lays out all the facts you need to know before choosing and setting up your own business
◆ highlights common problems and potential minefields in a new business

£7.99 Paperback 0 7494 1187 2
128 pages 1994

Great Ideas for Making Money

Niki Chesworth

◆ 70 inspiring ideas on making money from antiques dealing to window cleaning
◆ advice on how to turn your ideas into profits

£7.99 Paperback 0 7494 1188 0
224 pages 1994

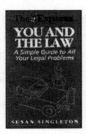

You And The Law

A Simple Guide to all Your Legal Problems
Susan Singleton

◆ a jargon free guide to remove the confusion surrounding the legal system
◆ practical advice on everything from tax and employment rights to divorce
◆ advice on how to deal with solicitors and legal actions

£6.99 Paperback 0 7494 1133 0
120 pages 1994

Available from all good book shops or to obtain further information please contact the publishers at the address below:

Kogan Page Ltd
Pentonville Road, London N1 9JN
Tel: 0171 278 0433, Fax: 0171 837 6348

your favour if the pound goes down, but against you if sterling rises. Investment experts say that getting the currency right can be more important than picking the right stocks and shares.

Equity unit trusts

The most common unit trust, and which is suitable for longer term investment, is the 'equity' fund. As the name implies, they invest your money in a wide range of companies' shares, and are meant to be held on to for at least five years. This is, in part, because the price of the underlying shares might vary widely during this time. If you decide on an equity unit trust, the number of options on the market is enormous. You can pick a fund designed solely to give you a good income, you can pick a fund that aims for capital growth. These can be suitable if you want an income that increases over time and you can opt for specialisations in industries or by a preference such as 'ethical' or 'green' funds.

Should you be looking for an income, there are UK Equity Income Funds that invest in UK shares paying high dividends, there are UK Growth and Income Funds that aim to provide a good income and increase your capital, there are also the self-explanatory International Equity Income Funds.

If you are looking for capital growth, options include UK Growth Funds, UK Smaller Companies Funds, International Growth Funds, Investment Trust Funds, which invest in invest-ment trusts (see Chapter 6) and any number of specialist funds. There are even Funds of Funds, which invest in the units of other trusts. With a 'fund of fund', the manager puts your money into a selection of the other trusts in the same stable. They are gener-ally considered a good 'starting' point for first-time investors.

Charges and further information

Most unit trusts have an initial charge and an annual manage-ment charge. Initial charges tend to be five to six per cent, which will be the difference between the price at which you buy the units and the price at which you can sell. This means that before you can start to make a profit on your investment, it must rise by five or six per cent. This is known as the spread, and covers initial commission as well as dealing fees when the plan manager buys the shares. Annual charges, which cover the running of the fund, are typically about 1.5 per cent. An increasing number of companies, though, are levying lower initial charges and imposing an exit charge instead, which will be high in the first year, and then gradually fall to nothing. Most cash funds have no initial charges, only annual management fees.

After you have decided which type of trust is best designed to suit your needs, you should decide whether you want to invest directly with the fund manager or through an independent broker. Many brokers will share their commission – usually 3 per cent with you – especially if you have already made up your mind so they only have to do the 'paperwork'. The Association of Unit Trusts and Investment Funds has produced a *User's Handbook* and a *Unit Trust Directory*, which lists unit trust management companies and authorised unit trusts. For a copy, write to: The Unit Trust Information Service, 65 Kingsway, London WC2B 6TD, or telephone: 0181 207 1361. There are also a number of magazines, such as *Money Management* or *Planned Savings*, which will give you tables of past performance figures, although you should remember that past performance is no indication of future gains.

7

Investing in Investment Trusts

If you wish to spread your risk when investing in shares there is an alternative to unit trusts – investment trusts. Investment trusts are companies that are quoted on the Stock Exchange, just like British Telecom or Hanson, but their business is to invest in other companies' shares. The first investment trust was created well over 100 years ago. Currently, there are over 250 quoted on the Stock Exchange, with combined assets of around £50 billion.

As with a unit trust, investment trusts help to avoid putting all your eggs in one basket. The big difference is the structure of the investment trust which can magnify gains when markets are rising, and, needless to say, increase your losses when the trust falls out of favour.

Unlike unit trusts, investment trusts are closed-end funds. This means that when the trust is set up, the managers decide in advance how much capital they want to raise, and issue a fixed number of shares accordingly. Then the law of supply and demand takes over. Unlike unit trusts, investment trust managers cannot just turn on the tap to issue new shares when they are popular, although new shares can be floated. These are known as 'C' or 'S' shares. Investment trusts also differ from unit trusts in that their price movements are dictated by different criteria. A unit trust's price will rise or fall depending on what is happening to the value of the underlying assets. An investment trust's price, on the other hand, will be dictated by supply and demand. No matter what is happening to the underlying shares, if a trust is out of favour and investors are selling, its price will fall. Another distinction from a unit trust is that if an investor wants to sell their stake in the trust, they do so on the open market, possibly through a stockbroker, rather than selling back to the trust manager.

This difference in what dictates the price movements often gives rise to a discount. This means that the price of the shares in an investment trust does not reflect the full worth of the underlying assets. Say an investment trust was trading at a discount of 10 per cent. That means that you would pay 90p to get 100p's worth of assets.

When investment trusts are very unpopular, as they were in the 1970s, the discount widens — in some cases to 40 per cent. When they are more popular, as they have been recently, the discount narrows to four or five per cent. When they become extremely popular, the shares trade at a premium, but this means that you could be paying 110p for 100p's worth of assets. Discounts can work in the investor's favour: if you buy at the right time, you can see the discount narrow, but they can also work against you if the discount widens. This discount also means that investment trusts are occasionally as takeover targets. A company buying up an investment trust that has been trading at a discount will immediately have a range of assets that it bought at less than the market value. Of course, the same applies to you. If you buy £1,000 of 'net asset value' for £800, you still get the income on the NAV.

Investment trusts generally have a wider range of investment targets than unit trusts. Both can invest in the shares of quoted companies, but investment trusts can also put money into unquoted companies and property. They can even borrow money to buy more shares, a process known as gearing. Highly geared investment trusts are riskier than the more conservative variety; when the market goes up, their price will rise faster than standard trusts, but when the market falls their price will plummet sharply.

	£1,000 becomes[1]	
	Five Years	Ten Years
	£	£
Halifax Instant Access	1,191	1,734
Halifax 90-day account	1,265	1,979
UK unit trusts	1,827	2,687
UK investment trusts	1,947	3,218
Inflation[2]	1,138	1,562

Source: Money Management

[1] Figure include reinvested income after tax
[2] Inflation: the amount you need to keep the same spending power

Figure 7.1 How share-based investments beat inflation – and the savings account

As with a unit trust, there is an investment trust for you whatever your investment objectives. You can invest for capital growth, income, both, or in any number of specialised sectors, industries or countries. Investment trust novices who want a mixture of income and capital growth, are best advised to put their money into general trusts. These invest in a broad spread of UK shares or international shares, and comprise about 58 per cent of the money in investment trusts.

Capital growth can be gained in two different ways. You could invest straightforwardly in trusts in the UK and international growth sectors, focusing on a sector or geographical area that is to your liking. Or, if you are a more sophisticated investor, you could put your money into shares in split capital investment trusts or warrants (see below).

The same goes for those investing in income. You can buy straightforward income trusts, you could buy a growth trust and periodically sell shares, or you could look at split capital trusts.

Split capital investment trusts

Investment trusts can consist of any number of weird and wonderful permutations, which are more suitable for the experienced investor, and nowhere is this more obvious than in the split capital investment trust. These divide the gains or losses of the portfolio among different classes of investor according to their needs. Shares in split capital trusts have traditionally been divided into income shares and capital shares: the first to provide income and the second to provide capital growth. Shareholders do not reap the benefits of both, because they buy either income shares or capital shares. This is because if you buy income shares you may get very little or none of your capital back, and if you buy capital shares you may receive little or no income. If you buy 'units', which 'unsplit' the divisions and re-create the original underlying shareholdings, you end up with a 'balance'. However, there is little point in selecting a split level, some of which have as many as five classes of shares, unless you can use their special characteristics.

SCITs are established for a fixed period, after which they are wound up. Throughout the period of the trust's life, the income shareholders have the right to most or all of the fund's dividend income. When the fund is liquidated, the capital shareholders get most or all of the remaining capital.

Capital shares are suitable for higher rate taxpayers who want to get their gain as capital growth rather than income. The income shares, which usually provide a higher-than-average rate of return, are better for basic rate taxpayers. However, due to the potential for capital loss, they can also be higher risk.

Split capital trusts first appeared in the 1960s, and grew in popularity during the late 1980s. They currently make up 10 per cent of the market, but recently their star has waned as the fashion for 'financial engineering' has declined. They have also become a lot more complicated. Split capital trusts can now offer zero dividend and stepped preference shares, and hybrid trusts have recently appeared, which offer zero dividend preference shares with ordinary income shares. Zero dividend preference shares are suitable for cautious investors, who need a fixed capital sum at some point in the future, according to the AITC. They pay out no income, but offer a capital return that is fixed but not guaranteed. They have tax advantages for shareholders who are able to cash in on their capital gains tax features.

Ordinary income shares pay out all the income from the trust. However, shareholders will get no capital back until at least one other type of shareholder, usually holding zero dividend preference shares, has been repaid. This means that if you put a certain amount of money into a trust that is due to be wound up in five years, you will get an income for that five years, but you may not get any capital back at the end of it.

Stepped preference shares are also low-risk, but pay out an income as well as a fixed capital return, which is paid when the trust is wound up. They pay out dividends that rise through the lifetime of the trust at a predetermined rate.

Some split capital investment trusts get more sophisticated still: they offer units. The units are a combination of the two types of share. Sometimes the units are made up equally of capital and income shares, which means that they are very much the same as an ordinary share in a more conventional investment trust.

Due to the complexity of this type of trust, you should seek expert advice when buying.

Warrants

Some trusts also offer warrants, usually as a 'sweetener' along with new investment trust issues, although these are only suitable for the highly sophisticated investor. For a small price, the holder of the warrant gets the right but not the obligation to buy the trust's shares at a specific price and within a set time span, limited by what is known as the exercise date. If you buy a warrant costing 10p, which gives you the right to buy the shares at 50p and the price moves up to 100p, you have made 40p on your initial outlay — a return of 400 per cent. On the other hand, if the price of the share never rises above 49p, you lose the lot. Warrants can be traded separately from the investment trust shares and their price will be affected by the trust's share price movement.

Costs

Investment trust saving schemes are one of the cheapest ways of investing on the stockmarket. You pay monthly sums to the management companies, which can be as little as £20 a month. There are also schemes that allow you to make one-off lump sum payments of over £250. This is a good way to build up some capital and you can often vary or change the payments if you wish. Otherwise you will usually buy them through a stock-broker, in which case you pay commission, typically 1.5–2 per cent. Increasingly, companies are offering them direct to the public through savings schemes, which means you pay no commission at all.

The spread — the difference between the price at which you buy and the price at which you sell — also tends to be lower than with a unit trust, at about three per cent. On top of that, you pay 0.5 per cent stamp duty and annual management charges, usually 0.5–0.75 per cent.

As with a unit trust, investing through savings schemes is a big plus if the market goes down because pound cost averaging applies. Because you 'drip feed' funds into shares in the trust every month you avoid the risk of buying all your shares when the price is high. You receive fewer shares for your money when prices are high, but you benefit from buying more shares when prices are low.

If you want more information about investment trusts, *Money Management* publishes monthly performance figures. The Association of Investment Trust Companies publishes a series of free leaflets to help you on your way, telephone: 0171-588 5347.

8

The Gilts Market

Equities are one way of making money on the stockmarket; the other main opportunity is through buying gilts, bonds issued by Her Majesty's government. Gilts are one of the safest investments in one sense at least: they are issued by the Government through the Bank of England. It is extremely unlikely that the Government will go belly up in the way that the Polly Pecks, BCCIs and Colorolls of this world have done. Like stocks and shares, gilts are quoted on the market and their prices can also go down as well as up, which means that if the market moves against you, losses can occur if you sell before maturity.

The safety aspect of gilts is underlined by their very name — gilt-edged stock. The Government has never failed to meet interest and capital repayments and only the most pessimistic of observers would assume that it would be likely to do so. Gilts are issued when the Government wants to borrow money, so when you hear that the public sector borrowing requirement is on the increase, it is safe to assume that a new issue of gilts will not be far behind.

Gilts differ from equities in a number of significant ways. For one thing, they are bonds. Companies issue bonds as well, and do so for the same reason as the Government: to borrow money. When you buy a share in a company, you are doing just that — you become the holder of a stake in a company. When you buy a bond or a gilt, you are in essence lending the company or the Government money. That loan runs for a fixed period, ending at maturity and you are paid a fixed amount of interest on it. So what are you betting on?

What are you betting on in a gilt?

When you buy a share in a company, you are taking a bet on that group's success in growing its business and its profits. When you buy a gilt, you are gambling on the success or otherwise of the UK economy in the eyes of huge international investors who can literally move billions at the press of a computer button. They not only analyse the UK scene; they compare it and contrast it with similar bonds from foreign governments. And, as with any share, their concerns are what will happen in the future. The past is a closed book which no longer interests them.

Bond investors analyse huge amounts of data each day from all over the world. International bond markets are far larger than share markets even though they never make the headlines on the *Nine o'Clock News*. What they are essentially looking for is a return which they can depend upon and which will not be eroded by inflation. If they expect prices to rise steeply, they will want a higher interest rate which, in turn, means lower bond prices. But when they are confident that inflation is under control, they will be content with less. Although the absolute rate of inflation is very important, just as vital is whether investors believe that it will continue at that level.

They also compare the yield on gilts with that on 'risk-free' investments such as short-term deposits in the money market where they know that each £100 will produce £100 plus a stated amount of interest in a fixed time-span.

Furthermore, they look at the return on equities. They will ask themselves if the perceived higher risks in shares are adequately reflected in share prices. They may not even want to invest in shares – some pension funds need the security of a regular dividend cheque from the government – but they must still consider this in their calculations.

Finally, gilt investors look at the future prospects of the pound sterling. If the pound goes down in value, their holdings will be worth less compared with an investment in bonds in another currency, such as the dollar or the German mark. If they believe this will happen, they will want to balance that loss with a yield that is higher than those available elsewhere. The result is that gilt prices will fall. But if sterling looks as if it is gaining on foreign exchange markets, the opposite happens. That is why gilt and international bond markets are affected by political factors. A change of government could mean a new economic policy which will produce uncertainty. And that is the greatest enemy of good investment values.

Thanks to inflation and the long-term decline of sterling, a £100 holding in a British government gilt made in 1946 lost all but 2 per cent of its purchasing power over the subsequent 50 years.

Most gilts have a set period of time to run. They cannot be cashed in before their maturity date, but they can be traded on the stockmarket, which means that if the price goes up after you have bought them, you can make money from your invest-ment immediately. Gilt prices may rise when the stockmarket falls. This is partly due to the safety aspect: they become more sought-after in risky times. There are any number of types of gilts in issue: those due to mature in the next couple of years, those with a few decades to run, those linked to the rate of inflation, and those suitable for different types of taxpayers.

When you buy a gilt, you will know that you are getting a fixed rate of interest and at the end of the term a fixed capital repayment.

You can learn most of the important information about a gilt by looking at its title. Say, for example, someone gave you a holding of £1,000 nominal of 8½ per cent Treasury Loan 2007. The £1,000 is the amount that you will get when the stock matures in 2007. However, the holding may well change in value before that time — it could be worth £900 or £1,100 depending on how the market moves. As the maturity date nears, the value of that holding will get closer and closer to £1,000. The 8½ per cent is the amount of interest you will get every year on the nominal value of your holding. It is paid not on the actual value — £900 or £1,100 — but on the £1,000.

This 8½ per cent is known as the coupon, and will also affect the price of the gilt in the market. Interest payments are usually made twice a year.

Treasury Loan is just one of the many names given to gilts. Others include Treasury Stock, Exchequer Stock, Exchequer Loan, Funding Stock, War Loan and Consolidated Stock.

A more complicated example is the 14 per cent Treasury Stock 1998–2001. This is known as a double-dated stock. It means that the Government must redeem the stock in 2001 at the latest, but it can do so at any time from 1998 onwards, giving three months' notice. The advantage to the Government of doing this would be if interest rates were low and it could refinance itself at a lower interest rate than 14 per cent.

Gilts are divided into shorts, mediums and longs. Short-term gilts have between 0–5 years to run, mediums 5–15 years and longs over 15 years. There are also some undated gilts, which have no fixed maturity date, but none has been issued since 1946. However, these stocks still have a face value of around £3 billion, of which War Loan accounts for nearly two-thirds. Long-term holders who bought for patriotic reasons just after World War II have lost around 98 per cent of their money to falling values and inflation. However, more recent buyers could have made profits by purchasing when interest rates were high and selling when rates fell.

Gilt prices

You have to find out the price of a gilt to work out its full value. They are quoted in newspapers usually on the same page as stocks and shares. At first glance it appears to be more complicated than a share price. Gilts are quoted in pounds and fractions down to thirty-second parts of a pound – about 3p – per £100 of nominal stock, although quotes are expected to change to pounds and pennies.

The price quoted in the paper will be the mid-market price from the previous day, halfway between the bid (what you get if you sell the gilt) and the offer (what you pay if you are a buyer). If a gilt is trading at £100, it is known as 'par' – over £100 is 'above par' while smaller figures are 'below par'. For instance, Treasury 12½pc 2003-5 is trading at £128¹⁵/₃₂. Ignore the word 'Treasury' – most gilts are 'Treasury' or 'Exchequer' – and concentrate on the figures. The most important is that this is above par – and that should be a 'stop sign' for private investors.

The price, on a date between 2003 and 2005 to suit the government, must revert to £100, so you are guaranteed to make a loss if you are a long-term holder. You will get a high income, on which you pay tax, but you will not be able to offset your eventual capital loss. They are, however, attractive to tax-exempt pension funds. The reason the price is above par is that the original coupon of 12½ per cent is far higher than other interest rates on offer.

Gilt yields – three to choose from

The first yield – your mathematical starting point is the coupon – the annual interest on the nominal value. In our example, you receive a dividend of £12.50 for every £100 on your stock certificate – £6.25 every six months – in this case on 21 May and 21 November.

The second yield is the 'flat' yield – the income you receive in relation to the price you paid, ignoring capital gains or losses. It is relatively simple to work out: divide the coupon by the price and multiply by 100. In our example, it works like this:

$$\frac{12.5}{128.47} \times 100 = 9.73 \text{ per cent}$$

This also means that to get £12.50 annual interest payments on a nominal £100, you must pay £128.47.

The third 'yield' is the redemption yield which takes more into account than the flat yield. It is based not only on coupon payments, but also on the capital gain, or loss, of holding a gilt until its maturity date. In this case, the gilt matures in 2003–5, so you would actually make a capital loss by holding on to it until maturity: £28.47 on every £100 you bought. This yield assumes that the investor reinvests the income from the gilt by buying more of the stock at the same redemption yield. The redemption yield requires a computer or special calculator; or you can find it in some newspapers or from a stockbroker. In our case, the 'guaranteed' loss brings the redemption figure to 7.24 per cent.

Gilt prices are affected by both short-term and long-term interest rates. When interest rates are rising, gilts are going to look less attractive because you will be able to get a better return elsewhere in the market. This means that the price will fall, so that the overall yield comes back into line with other investments. Equally, when interest rates fall, the price of gilts will start going up again. Interest rates might rise and fall considerably over 20 years, all of which affects the price of the gilt as it heads towards maturity. Gilt prices are also affected by supply and demand, as well as tax considerations — under current legislation, gilts are exempt from capital gains tax.

It is not just current interest rates that affect the price of a gilt; it is also what the market thinks is going to happen to interest rates in the future. For example, if you had a 20-year gilt paying out 15 per cent and the market took the view that in 20 years' time interest rates would stand at 20 per cent, it is going to mark the price down considerably. In fact, long-term gilt yields tend to be a reflection of what the market thinks long-term interest rates are going to do.

Index-linked gilts

Gilts have one disadvantage that shares do not: your capital is likely to be eroded through rising inflation. When a rise in the Retail Price Index is announced, you may see an immediate fall in share prices. However, those prices will recover quickly unless there is something else wrong with the company, which means that the amount of your capital will rise alongside inflation. Shares are real things – factories, stores, software concepts.

That is not the case with most gilts. If you buy £100 nominal of stock, that is what you will get when the gilt is redeemed. It is clear that if you bought that stock 10 years ago, £100 is almost bound to be worth rather less than when you shelled out for your purchase as prices are almost certain to be higher. That is why gilts tend to do better in a low inflation climate than one where inflation is rising.

There is a way of guarding against this: through index-linked gilts. These are gilts where both your capital and your interest payments are adjusted according to the Retail Price Index (RPI). Bear in mind that in the extremely unlikely event that the RPI actually falls over the life of the stock, then the value of your capital and interest payments will also go down. This will, however, be in cash terms rather than real terms as your purchasing power will be unchanged.

When you are looking at the price of index-linked stocks, some newspapers will show an index number written in brackets. This is known as the base index, the level of the RPI eight months before the stock was issued. The value of interest and capital repayments is calculated by comparing this with the index number for the RPI eight months before payments are due. That delay means that the cash value of the next interest payment (remember, they are made twice a year) is always known exactly.

Index-linked gilts tend to pay a lower rate of interest than conventional gilts, but as already stated, under current legislation they are exempt from tax on any capital gain. The return on an index-linked gilt is measured as the real rate of return, assuming two future levels of inflation. This form of measurement applies only to index-linked gilts and not to conventional gilts.

Buying your gilt

There are three principal ways to buy a gilt: directly from the Bank of England when a new stock is issued, through a stockbroker or bank, or through the National Savings Stock Register (also known as the Post Office Register).

When a new stock is about to be launched, prospectuses are published in the newspapers, as they are for a new equity issue. You can also be on a mailing list for details of new issues: if you wish to do so, write to: Bank of England's Registrar's Department, Southgate Street, Gloucester GL1 1UW.

The large issues are usually sold by auction. Although these auctions generally attract the attention of large institutional investors, they are also open to private individuals who can make non-competitive bids. The minimum you can bid for is £1,000 of stock (remember, this is the nominal value: the actual price might be higher — or lower), and the price you pay will be the average paid by professional investors. This means that you will actually get a better price than some of the big institutions.

The alternative to an auction is a public offering by tender. That means that the Bank of England will set a minimum price for the stock, but will invite the market to bid higher. When it has received all the bids, it will set an allotment price that all successful tenderers will have to pay.

New gilt issues often resemble the privatisations as they are launched on a partly paid basis. That means that there will be an initial down payment, followed by a series of further payments, known as calls, over the next few months. Until the gilt has been fully paid for, it is traded on a partly paid basis.

Should you make a non-competitive bid, you will be asked to enclose a cheque for £100 per £100 nominal bid, or less if it is a partly paid stock. If the ultimate price is less than £100 you will get a refund, and if it is more you will be asked to pay the difference.

If you have bid successfully, you will get a letter of allotment, and when the stock is fully paid, your holding will be registered at the Bank of England. Or, if you wish, you can ask for your holding to be registered on the National Savings Stock Register (see below).

Purchasing an existing gilt through a stockbroker is exactly the same as buying a share, but you will have to pay commission. The only difference is that settlement of the transaction is much faster; it usually happens the following day. That means you will have to get the cheque to your broker immediately, or make sure that you already have sufficient funds with them to cover the deal. That also means that if you are selling, you should receive the proceeds almost immediately.

Instead of going through a stockbroker, you could also buy and sell through the National Savings Stock Register (NSSR). The NSSR also charges commission, but at very competitive rates. It costs 0.7 per cent for the first £5,000, with a minimum £12.50 payment and £35 plus 0.375 per cent on amounts over £5,000. There is no minimum payment on sales.

If you want to deal through the NSSR, forms are available at Post Offices. You should check that the gilt you want is available (Government Stock leaflets will give you the relevant information), and you can either invest a fixed sum of money or buy a specified amount of stock. The stock is registered on the NSSR, and National Savings, rather than the Bank of England, send out interest payments. Stock held on the NSSR can only be sold through National Savings. This could be a disadvantage if you need to deal quickly.

However, holding stock on the NSSR can be a bonus for non-taxpayers as interest is paid without tax being deducted, though tax payers remain liable to pay UK tax. The maximum you can invest on any one day through the NSSR is £25,000, and there is no overall limit to your holding.

If you buy or sell around the time when the coupon payment is due, the situation is similar to that of a shareholder. Interest is paid if you are the registered holder of a gilt 37 days before payment is due. If you sell after that time, but before the actual payment date, you have to pay some of it to the buyer. You do not send a cheque; rather, this payment will be reflected in the price at which you sell.

Unlike shares, if you buy a gilt before that 37 day period, you will have to pay for the part of the interest payments that have already accrued.

Tax

Interest on gilts is subject to income tax, but profits or losses when selling gilts, or when they reach maturity, are not liable for either income tax or capital gains tax. As was said earlier, the inflation proofing of the capital amount is tax free.

If you hold gilts on the Bank of England Register, 20 per cent income tax is deducted at source before it is sent out to you. Holdings on the NSSR do not have tax deducted, but you must declare the interest payments on your income tax return.

Unlike share buying, no stamp duty is payable on purchases of gilts.

If you hold over £5,000 of gilts, you might have a tax liability on the interest payments. You do not have to pay tax on the interest that has accrued (and which you have paid for) before you bought the gilt. However, if you are selling, you will have to pay tax on the amount of interest that you have sold.

To find out more about gilts, the Bank of England's booklet, *Investing in Gilts: A guide for the small investor* is available free of charge, telephone: 01452 39 87 20.

9

How to Beat the Tax Man

'Nothing can be said to be certain except death and taxes', wrote Benjamin Franklin in 1789. Although it is true that just about all of us have pay taxes in some form or another, there are some ways of saving and investing where no tax is charged, or there is tax relief. Remember, though, you should never invest in anything simply for potential tax savings — if you save on tax but your money is eaten up in charges, there will be no ultimate benefit, or you lose money by picking the wrong investments.

Personal equity plans

The best way of investing in equities without paying tax is through a Personal Equity Plan (Pep). Peps were introduced in the 1986 budget by the then Chancellor, Nigel Lawson, but due to a combination of factors — high charges, a maximum investment amount of £2,400 and the 1987 stockmarket crash — until the rules were eventually relaxed to favour unit and investment trusts, the rules had been considerably relaxed and Peps are now one of the most popular ways of investing in the stockmarket.

You pay no capital gains tax or income tax on Peps, which makes them especially attractive to people who exceed the annual capital gains tax limit – £6,500 in 1997–98 – and to higher rate taxpayers. As you will never pay any income tax on Peps, this makes them an ideal investment for long-term retirement income planning.

There are now nearly 1,000 Pep schemes available to the investor. Over four million people have invested in one.

There are two kinds of Peps: general Peps and single company Peps. You are currently allowed to put up to £6,000 a year into the former and £3,000 into the latter, which means that you can stash aside £9,000 a year on which you pay no income tax or capital gains tax. And as married couples are treated separately, together you can invest up to £18,000 a year.

You are allowed to invest the full £6,000 in unit trusts or investment trusts through general Pep plans as long as they are at least 50 per cent made up of UK or EU equities. These are known as fully qualifying trusts. If they are not fully qualifying — that is, made up of less than 50 per cent UK or EU stocks — the maximum you are allowed to put in to a Pep is £1,500. However, within the same scheme, you can top up to the maximum £6,000 with fully qualifying funds. You cannot hold investment trusts or unit trusts in single company Pep plans. You are allowed to hold corporate bonds, convertibles and preference shares in a Pep.

Charges can vary quite significantly. Most unit trust Peps will have an initial charge of about five per cent and an annual management charge of between 1–1.5 per cent. Although something of a mini-price war seems to have started: some management companies levy no initial charge, but impose a sliding scale of early withdrawal penalties if you cash in your investment early.

Unit trust Pep holders will generally pay exactly the same fees as though they had been holding the unit trust outside the Pep. Self-select Pep holders should pay around one per cent as well as commission on share deals and standard charges for any unit or investment trusts.

Peps are available for every need: capital growth, income, a combination of the two, specialised sectors and geographical areas, so when choosing it is best to seek independent financial advice unless you are an expert. It should be emphasised that Peps are equity based instruments and are not without a certain degree of risk; if the market falls, then so will the value of your Pep. As with most equity investments, you should ideally hold it for at least five years.

You can invest even if you only have a small amount to save. Many companies now run monthly savings schemes for as little as £25 a month.

You can also run a self-select Pep. The plan manager still does all the administration, but you decide what shares you want to go in it. Self-select Peps are like a tax-free share dealing scheme. Costs vary immensely and may outweigh your tax saving, especially if you deal frequently. They do require a much greater knowledge of the stockmarket. If the firm gives advice, but leaves the final decision up to you, it might be called an advisory Pep.

Financial adviser Chase de Vere's *Pep Guide* costs £12.95, telephone: 0171 404 5766 for more details. The Prudential has published an *Introduction to Peps*, for a free copy telephone: 0800 000 000.

Tax Exempt Special Savings Accounts (TESSAs)

TESSAs were introduced in the 1990 budget by the then Chancellor, John Major, at a time when consumer spending seemed to be running out of control. TESSAs were meant to be a way of tempting savers back to the building societies, and when the first plans opened in January 1991 they were immediately and hugely successful, but not for the reasons the government hoped. Around 80 per cent of Tessa money was simply cash moved from taxed accounts.

TESSAs run for five years. Overall, you are allowed to invest £9,000: £3,000 in the first year, £1,800 a year in the next three years, and, if you have put in the maximum amounts, £600 in the final year. If you have invested less than the maximum amounts every year, you can put up to £1,800 into the account in the final year.

The first TESSAs matured in 1996. When a TESSA finishes its life, it can be 'rolled over'. If you have built up £9,000 in your account, you will be allowed to invest it all in a new TESSA within six months of the old one maturing, although you will not be able to reinvest the interest. If, however, you are a new TESSA investor or have less than £3,000 in your account, you will have to abide by the old rules and build up the £9,000 over five years.

On 1 December every year you may withdraw net interest, which will have been credited to your account, but you must not touch the capital. If you do, you have to close down the TESSA. If you leave the capital alone, gross interest will be credited to your account at the end of the five year period.

You can transfer your TESSA, capital, gross interest and all, to another bank or building society, but many will levy penalty charges. If you close the TESSA down early, you will only receive net interest.

You are only allowed to hold one TESSA at any one time, which means that unlike Pep schemes, you cannot get a new TESSA up and running every year. When you open one you are asked for your National Insurance number to ensure that you are not holding two TESSAs, and they are not open to minors.

Interest rates have fallen considerably since TESSAs were first introduced. Many banks and building societies paid around 15 per cent when TESSAs first came out. But rates soon fell, leaving many investors angry that they had little control over interest levels as there can be penalties, as well as the loss of tax relief, for ending a plan early.

Many fixed rate TESSAs are now available. These may be more suitable as investors can take a view on interest rates over five years, rather than feel they have been 'suckered' in by a high rate, only to see their returns fall once the bank or building society decides it has attracted enough money.

National Savings

The Government offers a range of tax-free products through National Savings. These are some of the most secure investments on the market, as they are backed by the Treasury and are literally as safe as the Bank of England. As with equity-based plans, most should be seen as five-year investments, and are not suitable as short-term alternatives to bank and building society accounts.

National Savings offers four products that are not subject to capital gains tax or income tax, but you do have to pay inheritance tax on them as part of an estate. Unlike TESSAs, you do not lose the tax-free benefit if you have to cash in early, but you will see lower returns as interest rates only build up to their full level over the product's entire life. All, except Premium Bonds, offer a guaranteed rate of return.

The higher your tax rate, the greater your benefit on the tax savings, as with other forms of tax exemption. For instance, a 6 per cent tax-free rate is worth 7.5 per cent to a basic rate taxpayer and 10 per cent to a top rate taxpayer.

Index-linked savings certificates

The value of the certificates is index linked to match changes in the Retail Prices Index, which effectively makes them inflation proof. You also get guaranteed extra interest if you hold the certificates for five years.

The certificates work like this. If you invest £100, and the rate of inflation after you have held them for a year is 2.3 per cent, your holding automatically increases to £102.30. On top of that, you will get interest on the purchase price. The whole of that new amount will earn further index-linking and extra interest in the second year, and so on.

When the five years are up, you can either cash in your certificates or reinvest them in a new series. Currently the minimum investment is a lump sum of £100, and the maximum is £10,000 plus up to £20,000 if reinvesting matured certificates, which means that you can have £30,000 invested in total.

You can cash in all or part of your investment early, but you will earn a lower rate of extra interest. You will only get your money back if you cash in your certificates in the first year.

Savings Certificates

These certificates offer higher guaranteed annual rates of interest.

Over the five years, the current return is equal to 5.85 per cent compound interest a year. The minimum investment is a lump sum of £100, the maximum is £10,000 plus the £20,000 reinvestment allowance from previous issues. You can cash in early, but you will get a lower rate of interest. Reinvestment certificates repaid before the first anniversary of purchase earn four per cent a year for each complete three months held. For other certificates, you get nothing more than your money back if you cash them in during the first year.

Children's bonus bonds

As the name implies, these are suitable for children under the age of 16. You need to have a lump sum of £25 to invest. At the end of each year, interest is added and at the end of five years a bonus is added. The plan can carry on until the holder is 21, when the final bonus will be added on.

The maximum holding is £1,000. Anyone over 16 can buy these bonds for anyone under 16. They can be cashed in without notice at the five-year bonus date, or when the holder is 21 or over. At other times one month's notice is required. No interest is earned on bonds cashed in within a year. If the bonds are cashed in before the holder is 16, the money is repaid to a parent or guardian, otherwise the holder can apply.

Premium Bonds

Go on, have a flutter, says National Savings' marketing literature. ERNIE, Britain's best-loved electronic wizard, now creates one millionaire a month — tax free.

Minimum investment is £100 and the maximum is £20,000. You do not earn anything on your money, but you do get the chance to earn the following range of monthly prizes:

- 1 prize of £1 million
- 4 prizes of £100,000

- 7 prizes of £50,000
- 15 prizes of £25,000
- 38 prizes of £10,000
- 75 prizes of £5,000

At the time of writing, there are also around 350,000 other prizes between £50 and £1,000.

The bonds go into the prize draw after you have held them for one complete calendar month following the month of purchase, and you can withdraw your money at any time. The return is twice as high as the National Lottery. The money you bet on Premium Bonds is the interest you forego. This is currently £47.50 for each £1,000 of bonds – worth £59.40 for a basic rate payer and £79.20 for a top rate payer. All that money goes in prizes. But were you to buy one National Lottery ticket a week for a year, spending £52, only around half that goes into the prize fund.

For more details on all these and other National Savings products, leaflets are available from the Post Office or telephone: 0645 645 000 during office hours. The calls will be charged at local rates.

Enterprise investment schemes (EIS)

EIS schemes appeared at the beginning of 1994 as a replacement for Business Expansion Schemes. They pander to every investor's dream: to get in at the start of a Body Shop type success. However, EIS schemes are extremely risky, and the only money that you should put into them is money that you can afford to lose.

For More Flexible Tax Free Investment, Phone Sharelink – 0121–233–9955.

EIS schemes allow you to invest up to £100,000 in a fledgling company, on which you can claim tax relief at 20 per cent. You can also invest proceeds of another investment that would otherwise have been liable to capital gain in an EIS and defer the capital gain charge, which means that you could get initial tax relief of up to 60 per cent.

The company itself is only allowed to raise up to £1 million through an EIS scheme — not very much for most businesses nowadays. And EIS schemes are banned from running private rented housing schemes — the kind of businesses that made some BES schemes such a success – although even a London strip joint has raised money through this plan.

Many small companies go under within a few years of setting up, so you should be extremely careful when looking at EIS schemes. If your chosen entrepreneur's brainchild goes under, you will not get a penny back. For further advice, consult a specialist financial advisor.

Venture capital trusts (VCTs)

Another innovation in the 1994 Budget, VCTs resemble a combination of an EIS and an investment trust. VCTs are companies that are quoted on the Stock Exchange, and at least 70 per cent of their investments must be in unquoted trading companies, with not more than 15 per cent of the trust in any one company. They operate on the same principle as an investment trust — allowing the investor to spread their risk. Like an EIS, they allow you to claim tax relief at 20 per cent on £100,000 if you hold shares in the trust for at least five years. These trusts are not for 'first-time' investors.

Phone Sharelink for a PEP Talk – 0121–233–9955

Net yourself a tidy sum with a ShareLink self-select PEP.

If you like to play the market, and you appreciate the intricacies of investing, why hand your PEP to a fund manager, when you could leave it in more capable hands. Namely your own.

With a ShareLink self-select PEP, you take control of your investments, while we take care of all the hassle. You can invest up to £9,000 each tax year. That's £6,000 in a General PEP and a further £3,000 in a Single Company PEP.

You're free to choose which shares go into your PEP, free to buy and sell within your PEP, and free to transfer existing PEPs from this or previous tax years.

What's more, as you can hold all your General PEPs in one plan, you will only pay one low administration fee.

To find out more about our self-select PEPs, call us now on

0121 233 9955
Quoting reference DEG

Do it now, and net yourself a tidy sum.

SHARELINK

SAVE WITH DIRECT LINE FINANCIAL SERVICES

As you have read through the Investment Guide you will have come across sections on regular and lump sum savings. If you'd like a product that is straightforward with no frills attached, extremely competitive rates of interest and definitely no hidden charges - Direct Line Financial Services is the place to look.

Direct Line Tracker PEP - investment made easy

The Direct Line Tracker PEP lets you benefit from Stock Market performance tax free, as all income and capital growth earned on investment in the PEP is completely free of tax, and has a greater potential for growth than with bank or building society deposit. As it is a Direct Line product, it is extremely good value, simple to understand and highly flexible. The Direct Line Tracker PEP is sold on an execution basis only i.e. we cannot give you any financial advice when you phone up to buy the PEP.

How your PEP works

When you invest in the Direct Line Tracker PEP, your money buys you units in a unit trust. The unit trust invests in shares in the companies in the FT-SE 100 Share Index.* Companies share their profits by paying a dividend. Dividends received by the unit trusts are used to buy more shares. In addition, the tax on these dividends, reclaimed on your behalf, is reinvested to buy more units. Your PEP will also be free of capital gains tax on any growth in the value of the units.

Performance

As for performance, index tracking is definitely a good idea. Our surveys show that over 5 years while the FT-SE 100 has grown by over 100%, nearly 9 out of 10 funds have failed to match this performance. The Direct Line Tracker PEP has certainly reflected the benefits of index tracking with a 14% rise in value in its first 10 months.*

You have the choice of investing lump sums, regular monthly payments or a combination of the two. If you save lump sums, your first investment must be £500 or more. After that you can make top up investments of £200 or more whenever it suits you. With regular monthly savings, you can save as little as £30 each month. You can suspend your regular payments on request but must always have at least £50 in your fund. The most you can invest in any general PEP is £6000 each year.

While PEPs are generally regarded as a long term investment, we recognise that there are times when you may want access to your money. With the Direct Line Tracker PEP you can withdraw all or part of your investment at any time.

If you would like further information or would like a copy of Direct Line's PEP Terms and Conditions, please call us on 0181-253 7737.

* Source Micropal 31/12/96 UK Growth & Income funds, offer to bid basis with gross income reinvested.

Finally, the value of the units in your PEP and income from them, will rise and fall as share values and income levels in the FT-SE 100 Share Index fluctuate. This means that you could get back less than you invested. While the stock market has outperformed building society investment in the past, this is no guarantee of future performance. Tax reliefs amy be subject to future statutory change and value of tax savings and the eligibility to invest in a PEP will depend on individual circumstances.

10

Sharesave Schemes

Is your employer's company going places? And does it have quoted shares? If so, another way of becoming a shareholder is through Sharesave schemes, also known as Save As You Earn (SAYE). These schemes are not open to everyone — only employees of a company that runs one.

Sharesave schemes are a combination of a savings account run by a bank or building society and a share option scheme. They are quite easy to understand: you invest a fixed amount in the account over a fixed number of years. At the end of the term, you can either take the cash as a tax-free lump sum or use it to invest in shares in your company. The price of the shares will have been fixed when you enter the scheme and you pay no commission on the purchase.

Eligibility

To be eligible to join a Sharesave scheme run by your employers, you must meet a number of criteria. These will commonly include the length of the time you have worked with the company, usually at least one year, the number of hours you work per week and residence in the UK.

If you join the scheme, you are allowed to save between £5 and £250 a month in multiples of £1. If you are paid weekly, you can save between £1.25 and £62.50 a week in multiples of 25p. After five years you get a tax-free bonus equal to nine months' payments, and after seven years you get a further tax-free bonus equal to nine months' payments, bringing the bonus up to 18 months in total. This is equivalent to an annual compound interest rate of 5.53 per cent tax-free over five years or 5.87 per cent tax-free over seven years.

Options

You then decide whether you want the option to buy the shares after five or seven years. If you opt for the bonus after seven years, you only need make payments for five years; after that you can leave the money where it is without contributing anything further. However, if you do this, you will have lost the option to buy the shares. When the set period comes to an end, you can take the whole sum in cash, use it all to buy shares, or take part in cash and use the rest to buy shares.

The price at which you can buy the shares is fixed from the start. Many companies will fix the price by taking the average of Stock Exchange closing prices for a set number of days before the option is offered and then deducting 20 per cent.

- You choose: a 5 year scheme
- You save: £40 a month
- Total savings (£40 × 60 months) = £2,400
- Tax free bonus after 5 years = £360 (equal to 9 months' payments)

At the end of five years, you have a total of £2,760, which you can take in cash, use to buy shares, or a combination of the two.

To decide your next course, you should look at the current price of your company's shares. If it has risen and you choose to buy at the price fixed five years before, you make an instant profit. Alternatively, if it has fallen, you simply keep the savings and the tax-free bonus. Remember, if you do decide to buy the shares, their value might fall at a later date. Most options are worthwhile as there are few instances of shares falling back after five years, especially with a 20 per cent discount. If you sell, don't forget to consider stockbroker costs.

Monthly payments are deducted straight from your salary. Ideally you should not miss out any payments, but you can suspend payments for six months if you have to. The six months will be added on to the five- or seven-year period. And you cannot change the monthly amount once you have started saving.

When you are granted an option to buy the shares, you will receive an Option Certificate. If you decide to exercise that option, you complete the form on the back of the certificate and return it to the relevant address. You must exercise your option within six months of the five- or seven-year period or it will lapse.

Under certain circumstances, you can exercise your option early. These include retirement on your contractual retirement date, or if you have to leave your job because of illness, disability or if you are made redundant. If you take early retirement, some schemes will allow you to take your option, but usually you must have been in the scheme for at least three years.

If you leave the scheme under any other circumstances, your share option will lapse and you will forfeit the tax-free bonus. If you leave the scheme in the first year you will get nothing back except your capital. If you withdraw from the scheme in years 2–5, you will get three per cent tax-free interest on your investment. If you die within the five- or seven-year period, the inheritor of your estate may exercise your option within one year of your death. If you die within six months after the set period has ended, the inheritors have one year from the end of the scheme to exercise the option. Schemes are run for companies by banks and building societies. You should approach your employer if your firm has an option plan.

Tax

Interest earned on the account throughout the fixed five- or seven-year period and the bonus paid at the end are not liable to income tax or capital gains tax. You also do not need to pay income tax when you are granted the option to buy shares or when you exercise that option. But if you sell the shares, you might be liable for capital gains tax. You can, however, transfer the shares into a single company Pep within 90 days of exercising your option without paying CGT.

11
Finding a Stockbroker

Now you know all about shares, it's time to find a stockbroker. There are about 150 stockbrokers who deal with private clients throughout the country. For a comprehensive list, write to the Association of Private Client Investment Managers and Stockbrokers (APCIMS) at 112 Middlesex Street, London E1 7HY. APCIMS, which has about 120 members, will send you a booklet detailing services and sometimes charges offered by the brokers, as well as information about whether they have a minimum amount that they will deal in. Many banks and building societies now operate their own stockbroking service; you should go to your local branch for details.

When choosing a stockbroker, you must first decide exactly what you need from them. Most stockbrokers now offer three basic services: execution-only, advisory and portfolio management.

Execution-only

Execution-only is not as painful as it sounds! The stockbroker will buy and sell shares for you, but will offer no advice on the transaction. If you use an execution-only service frequently, you should make sure that you have the knowledge to back up your investment decisions. However, they are useful for one-offs like privatisation issues when you just want to sell the shares. Many brokers will offer special limited deals at knockdown prices in the case of a privatisation issue — watch the financial pages in the press for details.

Because of the limited service they provide, execution-only brokers are the cheapest to use. Transactions are generally done over the phone, and they will usually charge a minimum fee of, say £15, (sometimes less for the one-off privatisation deals), which will rise depending on the number of shares you have to sell. They can be cheaper if you opt for a slower postal service. Some brokers will offer 'family deals' if those sharing a surname and an address amalgamate their holdings. This can be useful for selling privatisation shares. On top of that, you will have to pay 0.5 per cent stamp duty on purchases.

Advisory dealing service

If you are an active shareholder, it is probably better to opt for an advisory service. This is more expensive, but it will provide you with whatever research facilities your broker may offer. These vary in scope and quality. The broker may have analysts who follow particular companies and publish research on the company's prospects, and this will provide you with information on which companies you should buy and why. They must declare any relationship with the company they recommend. Take care with 'licensed dealers' who try to sell you low-priced shares in companies you have never heard of. These firms – sometimes called 'bucket shops' – are even more dangerous when they call from abroad where they are not subject to UK investor protection laws. Some ask you how much you have to invest and then, via an illegal mechanism called 'churn and burn', take all your savings from you in extravagant 'dealing commission'.

At the end of the day when using an advisory service, the choice of which shares you want to buy and sell is up to you. Some brokers will only deal in minimum amounts starting, say, at £10,000, and some will want to make sure that you deal a certain number of times a year. When choosing an advisory service, you should always talk to the broker in advance about exactly what kind of service you want, what facilities will be on offer and how much everything is going to cost.

Costs vary widely, depending on the service you use. There will usually be a minimum charge of at least £15, and usually more. The charges will also be worked out depending on the amounts you deal in, and usually go up in tranches. For example, a broker might charge 1.5 per cent of the first £5,000, 1 per cent for the next £5,000, 0.75 per cent for the next £5,000 and so on.

Portfolio management

The third kind of service generally available is a portfolio management service. This is for really serious investors; it is a lot more expensive and provides a much higher level of service than the other two. Stockbrokers will generally require quite a high minimum investment for a portfolio management service, typically £100,000, although if you shop around you may be able to find a broker that will go as low as £10,000. There are two kinds of service: discretionary or advisory.

If you choose a discretionary service, your broker can buy and sell on your behalf without referring to you first; in other words, the management of the portfolio is up to him. You should, however, receive contract notes immediately afterwards detailing the transactions that have taken place.

If you opt for an advisory service, your broker will have to contact you for your approval every time a stock is bought or sold. Although you have greater control over the portfolio, this can be something of a disadvantage; if your broker sees a bargain on the market, it might have gone by the time he contacts you. This is in contrast to a discretionary service where

Sharedealing Made Simple –
Phone Sharelink on –
0121–200–2242.

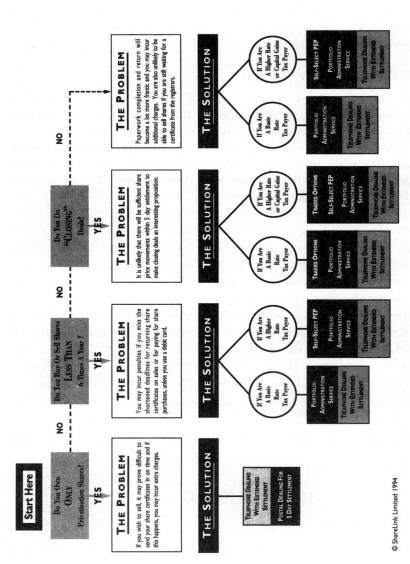

© ShareLink Limited 1994

Figure 11.1 How to Choose Your Stockbroker

your broker should obviously know exactly what your investment priorities are: whether you are building up a portfolio for
income or capital, for example, and exactly how much risk you
are prepared to take.

With a portfolio management service you will also get a
whole host of other benefits. These could include portfolio valu-
ations, as well as tax planning advice, information about the
stockmarket, collection and distribution of dividends, action to
be taken when rights issues, scrip issues and takeovers are
announced and the safe keeping of important documentation.
Many stockbrokers will also offer nominee accounts, which we
will look at in more detail in the next chapter.

Stockbrokers will also be able to provide information about
other ways of investing in the stockmarket, such as through
unit trusts, investment trusts and Peps as well as information
on the gilts market.

Choosing your stockbroker is always an important decision
and has become even more crucial now that rolling settlement
has been introduced (see Chapter 11). If you are an active
investor, you might have to lodge cash with your broker, which
makes it even more important to ascertain that your money is
in safe hands. If you have any worries at all, contact the
Securities and Futures Authority (SFA), which is responsible for
regulating brokers, at Cottons Centre, Cottons Lane, London
SE1 2QB (Tel: 0171 378 9000).

12

Paying – and Getting Paid – for your shares

There is a new way of paying for shares, and getting paid for shares sold, that has ended the 'gentleman's club' image of stockbroking. It is known as 'rolling settlement'.

Before rolling settlement came into effect, the Stock Exchange operated two- or three-week accounting periods, a system that had been in place for 150 years. No matter how many shares you bought and sold within that period, no money was paid out until the second Monday after the account period. The transactions were all handled in one go, for example, if you bought shares for £5,000 and sold them for £6,000, you would never have to pay the £5,000 and would in fact be owed £1,000. That meant that some speculators could buy shares even if they did not have the money to pay for them, watch the price rise and sell them again without having to pay out a penny, a process known as account trading. Of course, if they failed to gain enough to pay the broker's commission, they had to fork up their own cash. Sadly, most 'account trades' were losers.

Under the new system of rolling settlement, each transaction is handled separately and instead of a breathing period of up to three weeks, you must pay for the shares in five days. This will eventually fall to three days after you have bought them. This means that our speculator would actually have had to find the £5,000 as he would have had to pay for the shares before he was able to sell them again.

Nominee accounts

The way around this will be for investors who deal frequently to open a nominee account with their stockbroker. Nominee companies are set up for the purpose of holding shares on behalf of investors, and are the legal owners of the shares. The investor is the beneficial owner, and as such is entitled to receive dividends and other beneficial rights of ownership. Nominee accounts are run by stockbrokers, who carry out all the administration involved in owning shares. When the investor wants to buy or sell some of their holdings, the stockbroker will have the shares to hand and will be able to effect the transaction immediately.

Investors who use a nominee account may have to open a special cash account linked to the nominee account so purchases can be paid for immediately. They will usually have to pay a fee for nominee arrangements. They will neither receive annual reports and accounts and shareholder statements, nor be able to attend Annual General Meetings; these entitlements will be held by the nominee company. However, you may be able to make special arrangements to receive these rights, depending on your stockbrokers. Bear this in mind when choosing a stockbroker; some provide the service free, others will charge you. Shareholders might also lose out on the benefits of shareholder perks (see page 115), and so if you hold shares in the longer term in order to benefit from the perks, these should not be held in a nominee account.

However, nominee accounts really only apply to very active investors. Those with only a small number of shares who deal very infrequently will have other ways of avoiding high charges. Some execution-only brokers already allow investors to pay by using a Switch or Delta debit card and others are likely to follow suit. Some brokers may be able to delay the settlement date if you arrange to do so in advance.

Rolling settlement does not change the way you buy and sell shares — only the way you pay for them. Just as before, when you want to deal, you place your order, usually through a stockbroker, and receive a contract note confirming the transaction.

Crest

If you only hold unit trusts, or just one or two shareholdings, or you are so much in love with your shares that you have to have certificates as proof of ownership (even though you operate bank and building society accounts entirely trusting the computer), then you can skip this section.

But if you want to buy, sell and hold shares in a hassle-free environment with the possibility of annual or twice-yearly accounts that show all your holdings, their progress (or lack of it!) and the dividends you have received, in a form that is acceptable to the Inland Revenue (more important than ever with the advent of Self Assessment), then read on.

The stockmarket is doing away with share certificates, except for the small minority of small investors who want to hold on to them. They are being replaced by a scheme called 'Crest' which records your investments electronically in the same way as your bank balance. No one is being forced to give up certificates. And it may not make much sense for you to do so if you have just one or two shareholdings. Equally, if you have a greater number of separate shares, but you have adopted a buy-and-hold strategy so your dealings are very rare, you should stay with certificates.

The transition from paper certificates to electronic records for those who want it should be complete by mid-1997. Those on the system will find that buying and selling is speedier. For instance, you do not have to send a certificate in when you sell. This helps dealing over the phone or via the Internet. Speed is important as the standard length of time between striking a bargain and the settlement – your money being received or you getting payment when you sell – is being reduced to three days from mid-1997.

There are a number of Crest options, some of which are costly and are only intended for substantial shareholders with large investments in many shares. The most common choice for the private investor is the 'nominee' service from banks and stockbrokers. This means that your equity investments will be held in the name of the bank or stockbroker but in a separate account which will be yours and yours alone. If you combine that with a special bank account to pay for your purchases and receive payment for your sales, you will have an effort-free system with most of the paperwork taken care of for you.

Although there will be some hiccups as Crest beds down, it is here to stay. Stockmarket-quoted companies are moving to overcome initial problems, such as not sending annual reports to 'nominee' investors and not making share perks available to them.

LLOYDS BANK STOCKBROKERS LIMITED

48 Chiswell Street, London EC1Y 4XX. Telephone: 0171-562 6000. Fax. 0171-562 6001. VAT Registration No. GB 244 1555 76

CONTRACT NOTE

In accordance with your instructions we have BOUGHT   for the account of   ALAN BRIAN SAMPLE ESQ.

S A M P L E O N L Y

Bargain Date & Tax Point	Settlement Date	Bargain Reference	Client Code
27 JAN 97	10 FEB 97	ABC90001	SAMPLO001

Amount, Stock Description and Time	Price	Consideration
SECURITY 0140843		
100 BRITISH TELECOMMUNICATIONS	424p XD	£ 424.00
10:30 ORDINARY 25P		
COMMISSION (MINIMUM)	£18.50	
STAMP DUTY	£ 2.50	
TOTAL EXPENSES		£ 445.00

For and on behalf of
Lloyds Bank Stockbrokers Ltd.

*Member of the London Stock Exchange
and regulated by SFA*   E. & O.E.

A B SAMPLE ESQ.
1 SAMPLE STREET
SAMPLE TOWN
SAMPLE COUNTY
WX1 2YZ

For the purpose of Capital Gains Tax
it is recommended that this Note be retained

Subject to the rules, customs usages and interpretations of The London
Stock Exchange and/or the Exchange on which the transaction was effected

Lloyds Bank Stockbrokers Limited, a wholly owned subsidiary
of Lloyds Bank Plc, is Registered in England, No 2029332.
Registered Office: 48 Chiswell Street, London EC1Y 4XX

Figure 12.1 Contract Note and Tax Invoice

13
Fun With Shares

Playing the stockmarket is not a game — serious money is at stake. Neither is it all long faces and an anxious call to your stockbroker every morning. Share ownership can be enjoyable; it can bring you all sorts of unforeseen benefits, and you can get together with a group of friends to make the market work for you.

Shareholder perks

There are many reasons for owning shares: dividend income, capital growth and the excitement of building up your own portfolio amongst them. However, there is another reason: shareholder perks.

Like some credit cards and supermarkets which run loyalty schemes designed to win you over to their product, some companies run incentive schemes to persuade shareholders to spend as well as to invest with them. These are known as shareholder perks, and in a tiny number of well-publicised ferry companies can be as useful to the investor as the income or capital growth. Well over 100 companies run such schemes. Remember, you should not buy shares simply because of the perks that go along with them. The perks may mean little to you if you have lost all your money on the shares — and the company is at liberty to change its perks any time it wants to.

Some companies set restrictions on perks. You may be required to have a minimum holding of shares, or you might need to possess the shares for a certain amount of time.

The perks that are or have been on offer at various times include cut-price meals in restaurants and pubs owned by Allied Domecq, and discount coupons on airfares from British Airways for holders of 200 shares or more. P&O offers discounts on Channel crossings. Whitbread gives discounts on meals and wines. Scottish & Newcastle offers 30 per cent off selected cases of wine and whisky from subsidiary Waverley Vintners, and hoteliers, Resort and Stakis will give shareholders reduced hotel rates. Financial services company Great Southern Group will even give shareholders a discount on its Heritage Pre-paid Funeral Plans. Moss Bros gives shareholders a 10 per cent discount on a selection of clothes and shoes, although investors must have been on the register for six months beforehand. This stops someone from buying a few shares when they need a suit for a special occasion.

Barclays Stockbrokers has produced a free guide to shareholder perks, telephone: 0800 55 11 77 for a copy.

Investment clubs

So now you know all about owning shares: the only trouble is that you think you do not have enough money to buy any. One solution is to take out a regular savings plan putting aside a small amount of money to invest each month in unit or investment trusts. Another option is to join an investment club.

Investment clubs are groups of up to 20 people who pool their money to play the stockmarket. Typically, you pay an agreed monthly sum, say £20 or £30, which is pooled together and invested in the market.

One Call Is All It Takes – Phone Sharelink on 0121–200–2242

There are now an estimated 600 such clubs in Britain, and they are growing at a rate of about two a week. If you are thinking of starting your own club, ProShare, the body that promotes wider share ownership, offers a starters' pack, a video, a helpline and a monthly newspaper. The manual contains detailed information about how to set up a club, how to use a stockbroker as well as information about accounting and taxation. ProShare recommends that clubs should be made up of between three to twenty people and that members should raise about £500 for their first purchase, telephone: 0800 556 622 for further details.

Some stockbrokers also provide services for investment clubs. Barclays Stockbrokers, for example, has set up the Barclayshare Investment Club Service, which will provide either a straightforward share dealing service or will give advice on what to buy, telephone: 0800 55 11 77 for details.

Do not expect too much from an investment club, however. Despite the media interest they have generated, they will neither make, nor break, your fortune. Few achieve above-average results; many treat it as a way of investing in 'long-shot' shares while keeping a lid on their potential losses.

Investment clubs are really a social device where a number of people who have a common interest can get together for a few drinks and some intelligent chat. They are really no different from a chess club, golf club or Women's Institute.

14

Tax Without Tears

There are two taxes which can hit the investor: capital gains tax and income tax. We have already looked at investments that avoid these kinds of taxes altogether, but every investor will be subject to tax at some point or another, so it is worthwhile understanding the rules.

Capital gains tax

Every individual has an annual capital gains tax exemption of £6,500 (in 1997–98, but liable to change in every Budget). In other words, that is the amount of capital gain you are allowed to make each year before you become liable for CGT, which is charged at your highest rate of income tax.

The calculation of capital gains on the sale of shares is complicated. First, if you are selling part of a large holding built up over time, there are rules to identify which shares are being sold. You should seek professional advice if you are planning such a sale.

Second, if your shares have been held since 31 March 1982, you are allowed to assume that their value on that date is the cost you incurred when buying them. This might be useful to long-standing investors, as it could reduce the overall amount of your capital gain. Again, the rules governing this are complex, and you should seek professional advice.

If you make a loss on the sale of some shares, it can be set against your gains for capital gains tax purposes. Supposing you made a gain in one year of £20,000 and a loss of £10,000. Your overall gain would then be £10,000, which means that you would be liable to pay capital gains tax on that amount less your annual exemption. Had your gain been £1,000, you would not need the loss to bring it within the capital gains tax exemption. In this case, you would be allowed to carry the loss forward to use in future years if your capital gains exceed the limit then in force.

You can also reduce the amount of your capital gain through indexation relief. This is an allowance for inflation as measured by the Retail Price Index, and starts either at 31 March 1982 or at the date you bought your shares, if that is later.

However, since 30 November 1993, you have not been allowed to use this indexation relief to turn a capital gain into a capital loss or increase a capital loss; the most you can do is to reduce your gain to nothing. These rules apply equally to shares, unit trusts and investment trusts.

Income tax

When you receive a dividend payout, tax has already been deducted at 20 per cent. A non-taxpayer can get this refunded by the Inland Revenue. If you pay tax at the basic rate, your dividend income is treated as if it had already been fully taxed, even though the basic rate is higher than 20 per cent which means that you have nothing more to pay. However, if you are a 40 per cent taxpayer, you are liable for the full whack, which means that you will be charged an extra 20 per cent by the Inland Revenue.

Fixed interest stocks and permanent interest bearing shares

There are some kinds of investments that are treated differently for both capital gains tax and income tax purposes.

Fixed interest stocks (mainly gilts for the small investor) and Permanent Interest Bearing shares (PIBs) both pay interest after tax has been deducted at 20 per cent. Any profits made on the sale of gilts are not liable for capital gains tax. PIBs are building society shares listed on the stock exchange. You also pay no capital gains tax when you sell them.

Tax planning

Your tax situation may change with every Budget, so you should always remain alert to any further changes in the system. There are also a number of ways in which by planning ahead you can minimise your potential tax bill.

Another element to bear in mind is that married couples are now taxed separately which means that both have the full £6,500 annual exemption. They can also transfer assets between themselves with no capital gains tax liability, with the acquiring party being treated as if they had bought the asset at the same time and cost as the other. This means that if one partner has more than £6,500 worth of assets to sell, it might be worth giving them to the other partner first. Bear in mind that the Inland Revenue does not take kindly to tax avoidance measures, and may demand proof that the transfer was an outright gift.

Separate taxation also gives some leeway for income tax planning. The main point to bear in mind is that the partner with the lower tax rate receives all the income from investments. However, if you want your partner to receive dividend income, again the asset must be an outright gift and not capable of reverting to you. This applies to bank and building society dividend income, as well as to stocks and shares.

'Bed and breakfasting' is one common way to reduce your capital gains tax bill. It means selling shares one day and buying them back the next. That will either create a loss to set against your capital gains, or alternatively, establish a higher cost base on which future capital gains will be judged. Many stockbrokers will offer one-off cheap deals for bed and breakfasting.

Offshore investment

Offshore investment has had a rather shifty reputation. Traditionally one tended to think of investors who kept their money stashed away in the bank vaults of Liechtenstein and Luxembourg as not quite above board, and very likely to have something to hide. These days, however, most offshore investments are highly respectable.

It is important to distinguish between offshore investment and international investment. The first category is made up of the kind of investments that could be made in the UK, but are offshore for tax purposes. The second simply covers investments in overseas markets and will be looked at in the next chapter.

Most offshore investments these days are done through investment vehicles in tax havens very close to home such as the Channel Islands or the Isle of Man. You can have offshore investments in a building society, in a collective fund such as an Undertaking Collective Investments in Transferable Securities (UCITS), in other words an offshore unit trust, or in open-ended investment companies.

The main attraction of offshore investment is the tax advantage. Funds are not taxed at source as they are with deposits or unit trusts based in the UK. Most offshore investments now are either roll-up funds or have distributor status. Roll-up funds are those that roll up the amount of interest payable to the investor every year without necessarily paying it out. The payout comes when the investment is cashed in. However, the investor must pay income tax on the amount of interest that is being rolled up, whether or not the interest is actually taken. This does mean, however, that there is no capital gain to pay when the investment is cashed in.

Distributor funds are funds that distribute, or pay out, at least 85 per cent of their income every year. This will be liable for income tax, but the amount involved should be very small. Any gains when the fund is cashed in are liable for capital gains tax.

Phone Sharelink for a PEP Talk on 0121–233–9955, or turn to page 95

15
Looking Overseas

If the globe has become a smaller place, investment possibilities have grown. The world is, literally, your stockmarket oyster with possibilities from China to Chile.

There are plus and minus points about investing overseas. Some brokers hold that it is not necessary to buy directly into foreign markets as so many British companies have businesses overseas. Therefore, if you have a balanced portfolio of UK stocks then you are almost certain to have an international element.

However, if you are a serious investor, you really should have an international element in your portfolio, if for no other reason than to spread your risk. If the UK market plummets, it does not necessarily follow that overseas markets will follow, which means that your international investments might make up for disappointing performance back home. Major world stockmarkets tend to have short-term ups and downs in unison. 'When Wall Street sneezes, the world gets pneumonia,' they say. However, markets do diverge over longer periods.

There are a number of other reasons that you should consider investing overseas. One is that the UK market is a mature market, which means that although its ups and downs might seem alarming to the private investor, it is unlikely to zoom dramatically in either direction. This is not the case with emerging markets. Emerging markets are the economies that are just taking off, such as China, the Philippines, India and Latin America. They are much riskier than the UK, US and

Western European markets, but they also offer a much greater chance of doubling your money.

Then, of course, if you invest overseas, you get the benefit of expertise from stockbrokers and fund managers who specialise in the actual market itself. But as long as you aim for expertise, your funds are likely to do just as well if handled by a foreign-based fund manager than one stuck in the dealing rooms of London. It is down to the individual, not the location.

If you decide to look overseas, it is essential that you get expert advice. Talk to your stockbroker or independent financial advisor first, and remember that although the potential rewards can be great — the same applies to the risks.

Beyond our shores – in more detail

There is nothing to stop you investing directly in the shares of non-UK companies. Many private sharebuyers have holdings in well known international firms, especially American 'consumer brands' such as Coca-Cola or IBM. But putting your money into any overseas country is just as easy – in theory.

In practice, the major difficulty is that dividends are likely to be paid in the currency of the country where that company is situated, and that could cause problems and expense when you transfer that cash into sterling. But there are two ways around this. Some overseas companies have automatic dividend reinvestment schemes for those who require it, and if you have several holdings in one country, you can always open a UK or foreign bank account in the currency of that nation. This can be helpful if you visit that country often as you will then have a source of spending money.

Language, however, should not be a difficulty. Very large companies often produce versions of their shareholder communications in English as well as their own language, and there is a substantial amount of research in English on most international companies. If you wish to invest directly, it is best to stick to the largest firms in each country. Going further down the size scale could bring you trouble with registering the investment in your name.

But few private shareholders have either the depth of pocket or the breadth of knowledge to carry out the essentials of any overseas investment beyond the odd well known international blue chip – obtaining a diversified basket of shares.

To get a good spread of investments, you will need to invest through a unit or investment trust or through one of the new style Open Ended Investment Companies. You have a choice of well over 1,000 possibilities, so where do you start?

The easiest way in is through a general 'international' fund which spreads your cash around the world depending on how the fund managers see the international share situation. An investment in such a wide ranging trust is best for those who do not want to put all their faith in the UK stockmarket but have no fixed views on where else is attractive.

Most of these funds – and indeed virtually all the more specialised trusts investing overseas – are aimed at long term capital growth. Expect little in the way of dividends from any form of overseas investments in equities. Most foreign stocks give low income as there are other methods such as bonds and loans which are used in these countries to give a high dividend return. UK blue chips with their average of around 4 per cent in dividend income are the exception on the world stage rather than the rule. There are a few funds which aim at income from international shares but these have never proven widely popular.

The next stage of specialisation is the 'area fund' such as Europe, America or the Far East. Some, for example, America are dominated by one country – in this case the United States. But where there is a choice of several roughly equal nations, there is more than one way of spreading the investment cash.

The most common method is to decide on a percentage to go into each country – a European fund might put 20 per cent in each of Germany, France and Italy, 10 per cent in Holland and Spain with the balance spread among the other nations. Investment experts then compare this against the 'weighting' of each country. If French shares account for 20 per cent of the value of the entire European market, a fund which held 15 per cent of its assets in France would be 'underweight' and hence less optimistic, while an 'overweight' fund at more than 20 per cent would be considered an enthusiast for the French market.

This is known as a 'top-down' system, which means that the manager believes that understanding the relative strengths and weaknesses of the economy of each country is the most important starting point. If you believe, for instance, that conditions including the currency are good in one country, you overweight it before giving any consideration to the shares you buy. Some managers take the top-down concept a little further. They so believe that getting the country and currency right are the major factors for success that they simply buy an investment which tracks the major stockmarket index of that nation.

At the other end of the spectrum is the 'bottom-up' method. This ignores the country of origin of a company and concentrates on the future for that individual concern. With increasing emphasis, especially in Europe, on pulling down national barriers to trade, the success or otherwise of a company now depends on how it copes with the wider marketplace. A German company may sell throughout Europe and have plants in the UK, France and Spain as well.

The same, many argue, is also true of Far East or 'Pacific Rim' economies. They are so dependent on exports that their national background is of little consequence. A Singapore company making electronic equipment, for instance, will sell little of its product in its local market. The same may even be true of Australia, whose biggest companies are world players in natural resources such as metals and other mining products, and which have to sell against international competition at prices governed by world supply and demand.

Some Far East funds buy shares in Japan, others do not. Unit trust listings have separate sections for funds with a Japanese element and for those which avoid that country.

There are a number of 'one-country' funds covering Europe, the Far East, Latin America and situations varying from Russia to Israel and South Africa, but these have rarely proved very popular with UK investors. Many have been launched after the market they cover has already undergone a big upwards move. They then leave private investors exposed to the inevitable selling as the original professionals take their profits.

The professionals then move on to the next market they believe will emerge and hope to repeat the trick. It often works as long as they find a new stock exchange to 'transform'. A relatively small amount of international cash can transform a tiny market overnight. These professionals then need someone to buy the overpriced shares – and all too often that is the 'mug punter' through well marketed 'emerging market' funds.

One-country funds are, however, popular in two locations: the United States and Japan – the world's largest stockmarkets. Investing in the United States has generally been a worthwhile experience. It can be the first step outside the UK for many.

Japan, however, is different. It was 'discovered' by overseas investors in the 1970s, and by the end of the 1980s share prices had reached stratospheric, perhaps lunatic, levels. At that time, the value of the Tokyo stockmarket was worth one and a half times the combined worth of all the other stockmarkets in the world other than the United States. Even more ridiculously, the privatised Japanese telephone company NTT was valued more highly than the entire German stockmarket.

It could not last. The Nikkei index, the main measure of Japanese shares, which stood at around 40,000 at the end of 1989 slumped to as little as 14,000 a few years later, and at the time of writing it is still around half its peak value. UK investors did enjoy some cushioning, however, against the fall for much of the time thanks to the strength of the yen against the pound.

But more recently, the pound has fought back. That magnifies any problems in an overseas investment – unless you have put your money in one of the few 'hedged' funds which take the currency factor out of the equation.

Always remember that people selling funds have a job to do – to convince you to buy. They will not reveal negative factors other than a general warning common to all unit and investment trusts that past performance is no guarantee to the future. Conditions do change in countries, often as a result of growing wealth so that the second generation does not want to work as hard – or for so little – as their parents. You should always question stories about 'hot' investment areas by asking why the professionals, with all their ability to move money around the globe in an instant, have decided to leave the growth being forecast to the small investor.

Table 15.1 Performance in: UK pound sterling – Twelve months to 27 December 1996

	Currency Return	Price Return	Total Return	Hedged Total Return
	1 Year	1 Year	1 Year	1 Year
World		0.56	2.72	17.97
Americas		9.43	11.81	23.50
Brazil	–15.13	24.77	27.06	27.06
Canada	–9.72	16.04	18.70	33.17
Mexico	–11.19	6.85	8.30	8.30
United States	–9.27	9.00	11.38	23.16
Pacific Basin		–18.36	–17.37	4.35
Japan	–19.36	–24.41	–23.84	0.32
Australia	–3.12	5.95	10.48	12.80
Hong Kong	–9.30	18.66	22.70	35.98
Malaysia	–8.78	12.82	14.52	24.82
New Zealand	–1.94	4.53	9.15	7.64
Singapore	–8.25	–6.46	–5.22	6.57
Thailand	–10.86	–48.34	–47.11	–47.11
Europe		8.25	11.58	25.07
United Kingdom	0.00	11.45	16.10	16.10
Austria	–15.70	–1.28	0.56	21.54
Belgium	–15.94	–1.22	2.68	24.80
Denmark	–14.76	10.58	12.55	33.97
Finland	–14.52	19.13	22.06	44.74
France	–14.65	8.26	11.62	32.44
Germany	–15.73	5.31	7.23	29.78
Ireland	–4.19	16.77	20.83	26.74
Italy	–5.33	2.78	5.06	7.85

Netherlands	−15.91	11.84	15.40	39.93
Norway	−10.23	15.94	18.49	32.91
Spain	−15.38	20.72	24.92	43.43
Sweden	−11.93	22.65	25.47	41.40
Switzerland	−22.25	−8.28	−6.82	24.04
South Africa	−29.29	−25.02	−23.10	−23.10

Source: Goldman Sachs Equity Research.

Table 15.1, which comes from the major US and international investment bank, Goldman Sachs, shows four figures for each country over one year. It is designed for UK based investors who use the pound sterling, although the same source can produce similar exercises in other major currencies.

Currency Return shows the amount by which each currency has gained (a positive figure) or lost (a negative figure) against the pound over the twelve months. Remember a plus sign is good news for UK investors.

Price Return shows the gains or losses over the year in the index of the country in question used in this research. Many countries including the UK have several indexes such as the FT-SE 100 for major companies and the FT–Actuaries All Share for a far wider view of quoted concerns.

Total Return adds the effect of dividend income to the figure in column two. It will reduce negative figures and increase positive numbers. Total return figures of this kind always ignore tax considerations as these differ between investors as well as between different countries.

Hedged Total Return shows what would have happened to your investment if you had 'hedged', a device which removes foreign exchange fluctuations from the equation. Hedging brings costs and is only worthwhile if you think your currency is going to strengthen against that of the foreign currency. Hedged funds are rare in the United Kingdom as the pound has lost value over most periods and would therefore have provided poor returns to investors.

16

The Guardian Angels and Self-defence

With the best will in the world, you cannot guard against disaster. You can spend hours examining a company balance sheet under a microscope without realising that the chairman has had his hand in the till for years. You can put money into a bank without realising that widespread fraud is on the point of tipping it over. You can trust an investment advisor with all your funds, and discover shortly afterwards that he is living the life of Riley in an obscure South American state — on your money.

As far as straightforward investment in shares is concerned, when the price tumbles or the company collapses, your money, or most of it, has gone. But if you cannot guard against what a share is going to do, you do have some protection against the people who are running your portfolio — whether you have a large holding with a stockbroker, a small amount in unit trusts, or just a SAYE plan in the building society.

A series of guardians to watch over the investment industry was set up under the terms of the Financial Services Act 1986 (FSA) after a number of scandals convinced the Government that it was time to tighten up standards in the industry. There is a two-tier system of regulators: the Securities and Investments Board (SIB) and three self-regulatory organisations (SROs). These offer protection against fraud, but not against bad advice on which investments to pick. They can be slow.

Britannia do more to make investing easier.

It's not just investments that we go out of our way to help you with. At Britannia we pride ourselves in bringing you a wide range of financial products to suit your needs but without all the waffle.

With 140 years experience and the convenience of an extensive branch and cash machine network throughout the UK we're here to make sure all your finances run smoothly.

We also have the unique Britannia Members' Loyalty Bonus Scheme which demonstrates our commitment to sharing our success and profits with our members. Through the Scheme you can earn bonus points which are converted into a cash bonus at the end of each year.

If you're interested in a Building Society who'll bend over backwards for you then call in at your local Britannia branch or phone 0800 269 655 quoting code DEIG.

Lines are open Monday to Friday 9am - 7pm, Saturday 9am - 12noon.

The Sharing Society

Britannia Building Society, Britannia House Leek, Staffordshire ST13 5RG.

Your Bond for the Future

With savings rates at their lowest for thirty years, how can you ensure you are getting the best possible return without risking your hard-earned money - your security for the future - on speculative investments?

If only you could combine a guaranteed return of 8% gross p.a. from a high interest building society account with the potentially higher returns from the Stock Market .... all without any risk.

Well, that is exactly what is on offer from one of Britain's top building societies. Bristol & West has produced an investment package which combines the growth potential of the Stock Market, with such household names as Marks & Spencer and ICI, with the security and guaranteed return of a building society savings account. It was the first building society to design this type of product which appeals to a wide range of savers, whether they hold instant access accounts, TESSAs or PEPs etc.

In essence, the Bristol & West Balanced Guaranteed Equity Bond is two products rolled in to one:

One Year Bond: Part of your money is placed in a high interest building society savings account, paying 8% gross per annum fixed for one year (This issue closes on 3 December 1996 - the Society releases new issues throughout the year and the one year rate may change). At the end of that period, you can either re-invest the capital with the Bristol & West, the UK's eighth largest building society, or receive your funds in full.

Five Year Bond: The other part is invested for a five-year period in another building society account. This links the rate of interest paid on the investment to the performance of the FT-SE 100 Index. There is no ceiling on the level of potential earnings, but if the FT-SE 100 Index should fall - and we are aware that investments can go down as well as up - Bristol & West guarantees to return the original sum invested in full.

Basically, the Balanced Guaranteed Equity Bond gives you the chance to receive a potentially large return whilst not taking any risk with your capital.

Applying for a Balanced Guaranteed Equity Bond could not be easier - either call the number below or complete and return the coupon opposite for a priority application pack.

CALL 0800 20 21 21 FREE 24 HOURS
PLEASE QUOTE REF: DEIG

Life's Magic for the Motts

Margaret and Frank Mott have two passions in life - golf and their grandchildren, Richard and Lloyd. Margaret, 60, is a community care organiser for the Social Services in Skegness while Frank, 62, is a retired teacher. Both are keen to ensure their savings and investments are generating the best possible return, especially at a time when savings rates are so low.

"Margaret and I have a number of accounts", explains Frank. "As well as an instant access account and a TESSA, we also have some unit trusts and shares in Government privatisation issues.

"A couple of years ago, we decided to invest £2,000 in a Bristol & West Guaranteed Equity Bond. This gives us the opportunity to make potentially higher returns than a standard building society account by linking the rate of interest to the FT-SE 100 Index, reflecting the performance of the UK's leading companies".

Margaret enjoys keeping an eye each day on the FT-SE 100 Index.

"Share prices rose by nearly 20% last year and 11% so far this year (15 October 1996)," she says. "If it continues to rise we should make a handsome return on our investment."

Balanced Guaranteed Equity Bond - The Facts

* Five year investment linked to the percentage growth of the FT-SE 100 Index.
* No risk to capital - guaranteed
* No charges so all your investment is working for you. Investors in the Balanced Guaranteed Equity Bond do not have access to the dividends generated by the FT-SE 100 Index companies.
* Up to 50% of the total investment can be placed in one year bond - remainder in five year bond
* One year bond offers fixed rate of 8% gross p.a. and permits instant access to your funds. (The five year part of the Bond cannot be withdrawn for five years).
* Five year bond earns 100% of the percentage increase in the FT-SE 100 Index
* Minimum investment of £1,000 (into the five year bond).

Known as watchdogs, these four bodies are responsible for policing the financial services industry by granting authorisation to member firms, monitoring their progress and occasionally imposing fines or even closing down a firm that has not been carrying on its business properly.

Under the current system, the institutions effectively police themselves. There is still a debate raging as to how effective these watchdogs are, and whether it might be necessary for the Government to set up external bodies independent of financial companies to patrol the industry.

The act only covers investments and investment business, not deposits with banks and building societies, which are dealt with under the Banking Act and the Building Societies Act. Investments include shares, debentures and other securities, certain options and warrants and unit trusts and other collective investments.

Investment business includes dealing, managing, advising and the setting up of collective investment schemes. Almost everyone involved in the services defined under the act, be it an individual financial advisor or an enormous insurance company, must be authorised to carry on its business by the SIB or one of the SROs, who is then known as its regulator.

The watchdogs

Top dog in the investment business is the Securities and Investments Board. The FSA allowed for the establishment of an agency, the SIB, which was to be delegated most of the powers under the act. The SIB is now responsible for all the SROs. Most firms are, in fact, authorised by the other watchdogs, but if you telephone the SIB Central Register on 0171 929 3652, it can tell you who your company is regulated by.

When it was first set up, the SIB fell under the aegis of the Department of Trade and Industry, but since 1992 it has been responsible to the Treasury. Every year it reports to the Chancellor of the Exchequer, and that report is presented to Parliament. The SIB is a private limited company financed

Cautious investor seeking guaranteed returns?

A safer way to stock market investment.

For those who don't want to subject themselves to the vagaries of the stock market, NatWest has devised a series of Investment Bonds which offer returns which are guaranteed and generally ensure that your original capital is kept safe. In this way, they provide an ideal half-way house for those who want a better return than they are getting on their savings account, but who are not prepared to take the risks involved in other stock market investments. All the Bonds require a minimum investment of £5,000 and you need to be able to leave your money invested for the full term. Currently terms are between 2 and 5 1/2 years, depending on the type of Bond. There are options for income or growth.

The most popular bond in the range for people who want growth is proving to be the Guaranteed Growth Plus Bond. This promises to keep your original capital safe and offers a return which is linked to the rise in the FT-SE 100 - the index which charts the share price movements of Britain's top 100 publicly-quoted companies. This includes a guaranteed return which is currently 25 per cent* of your investment or 4.1 per cent per annum net to basic rate tax payers (roughly equivalent to the return you could expect on a savings account). This is paid out even if the FT-SE 100 Index falls, so long as the Bond is held for the full investment term, which is currently 5 1/2 years. If the FT-SE 100 Index rises sufficiently, the profit could be as high as 70 per cent*.

To further broaden the choice for investors, NatWest has just launched the Guaranteed Investment Fund linked to its Flexible Investment Bond, with a money back guarantee at the end of 5 years.

There is no fixed investment term and a minimum of £2,000 is required. The Bond offers the potential of worldwide stock market growth with no limit on the maximum amount which might finally be paid out.

You can find out more about NatWest's range of investment products and its Personal Financial advice service at a local NatWest branch or by calling 0800 255 200 for an investment information pack.

CALL 0800 255 200
MONDAY TO FRIDAY 8.00am to 8.00pm
SATURDAY 9.00am to 6.00pm

If you are disillusioned with the returns that your savings account is currently offering, it could be a very smart move indeed.

☘ NatWest
More than just a bank

entirely by the industry it serves; it does not receive a penny of taxpayers' money. That, say critics, is a serious weakness. The American system is paid for by the government and is far tougher – and more rapid in response.

The board is made up of practitioners and independent members, appointed by the Chancellor and the Governor of the Bank of England. The SIB's main aims are investor protection and promoting efficiency, which means that it imposes set standards of honesty, solvency and competence, and it has the power to bring criminal prosecutions. But these powers are rarely used. The SIB has been attacked for 'shutting the door after the horse bolted'.

The most important element of investor protection is the Investors Compensation Scheme. It is at the same address as the SIB although it is run completely separately and has its own telephone number: 0171 628 8820. The ICS is aimed at the private investor. It provides compensation if a firm goes bust, or if your investments have been wrongly handled and the firm itself is unable to meet a claim.

To get a payout under the scheme, the firm you have dealt with must be fully authorised by one of the SROs. The maximum you can get back is £48,000, that is, 100 per cent of the first £30,000 and 90 per cent of the next £20,000. The maximum the scheme itself can pay out in any one year is £100 million.

There are now three members in the second tier of the guardians. The first and newest is the Personal Investment Authority (PIA). Set up in July 1994, the PIA has taken over from the Financial Intermediaries, Managers and Brokers Regulatory Association (Fimbra) and the Life Assurance and Unit Trust Regulator Organisation (Lautro). Fimbra used to regulate independent financial advisors and Lautro used to be responsible for unit trust and life insurance sales people; now the PIA has taken over responsibility for them all.

As well as granting authorisation, it supervises and monitors its members, and has the power to impose fines or withdraw authorisation if a firm has been at fault. If you have a problem with a member of the PIA, there are two kinds of action you can take depending on whether you have a complaint or whether the firm has actually gone under. If the firm has gone bust, you might be eligible for compensation under the Investors Compensation Scheme. But if you merely have a complaint about how you have been treated, you could seek redress from the PIA Ombudsman.

The Ombudsman acts as an arbitration service if no other solution is available, and otherwise will attempt to conciliate between parties. If you have a problem, you should first try to sort it out with the company concerned. If this proves to be impossible, write to the Ombudsman. He is able to make awards of up to £50,000, and can make a recommendation that is higher than that, although both parties must agree to it. If the firm concerned is unable to pay the amount awarded against it, you might be able to get redress from the Investors Compensation Scheme.

There was some controversy about the PIA when it was set up, a debate raged about whether it should be controlled by industry insiders or consumer bodies. It has ended up more or less half-and-half, but there is still a lot of pressure on the PIA to prove itself more effective than Fimbra and Lautro. A great many people still believe the industry should be regulated externally.

The Securities and Futures Authority (SFA) is responsible for stockbrokers, futures dealers and traders. It cannot help if your broker simply makes a bad recommendation, but it can help if he runs off with your money. Like the other SROs, the SFA vets firms and individuals before granting authorisation. It has a complaints bureau to look at your problem, and an arbitration scheme. If the firm has gone bust or cannot pay up, you may have a claim under the Investors Compensation Scheme.

The Investment Management Regulatory Organisation (IMRO), is primarily responsible for regulating the large fund managers. Some of the firms used by small investors are regulated by both IMRO and the PIA, but if you have a problem with one of these, it is almost certainly the PIA that you will be dealing with. IMRO is now primarily concerned with the institutions.

Of course the SROs and the compensation scheme are there to clean up the mess after something has gone wrong. Ideally you should follow a few rules of thumb when investing which, with any luck, means you could avoid the problem in the first place.

They are:

- Always ask your advisor or sales person who they are regulated by.
- Ask how long they have been in the business and what kind of training they have had.
- Never buy anything you do not understand. Ask yourself if this type of investment really suits your needs.
- Never do business with a sales rep on a first visit; think about what he or she has said and investigate it.
- Do not respond to cold calls when an enthusiastic sales person rings you up out of the blue.
- Be highly suspicious of above-average rates of return.

Banks and building societies

Banks and building societies are treated entirely differently from fund managers, stockbrokers, independent financial advisors and so on. As they are regulated by the Bank of England and the Building Societies Commission respectively, they are not involved with SROS except when they act as appointed representatives of life insurance companies or own life insurance subsidiaries, which may be regulated by the SROs.

If you have a problem with your bank, you should talk first to your branch, and if you cannot resolve the problem, go to more senior management. If there is still an impasse, get in touch with the Banking Ombudsman.

If the situation is more serious and your bank actually goes under, you may be able to get some of your money back under the Deposit Protection Fund run by the Bank of England. This scheme allows you to get 75 per cent of your money (as long as it is in sterling) up to a maximum of £15,000.

Much the same applies to building societies: if there is a trivial problem, go to the Building Societies Ombudsman. There is also an Investors Compensation Scheme that will pay up to 90 per cent of your lost funds with a maximum of £18,000. Get in touch with the Building Societies Commission for more information.

There are many more advisors who do not fit in to any of the above categories as the main part of their business is not investment advice: solicitors and accountants, for example. They will be covered by one of the nine recognised professional bodies (RPBs) such as the Chartered Association of Certified Accountants, the Law Society and the Institute of Actuaries. There is a full list of the relevant addresses at the back of this book, as well as details of how to get in touch with all the bodies mentioned above.

Conclusion

So now you know everything you need for your steps into the investment world, should you rush out and stake your shirt on the stockmarket? No.

No one will ever really know everything about investment. And even the most experienced of stockmarket players can come a cropper: an awful lot of people have lost an awful lot of money in the crashes that have hit markets.

What you must do is to be sensible. Make sure that much of your cash is in safe investments, even if it means that you will not get as high a return as you could from shares. Do not invest large amounts of money in the market that you cannot afford to lose. Never be afraid to ask questions when you think you do not understand something.

And do not be afraid of investment. The value of investments can go down as well as up, but by careful planning you can always minimise your risk.

Sources of Further Information

Association of Investment Trust Companies
Durrant House
8–13 Chiswell Street
London EC1Y 4YY

The Association of Private Client Investment Managers and
    Stockbrokers (APCIMS)
112 Middlesex Street
London E1 7HY

Bank of England
Threadneedle Street
London EC2R 8AH

Bank of England's Registrar's Department
Southgate Street
Gloucester GL1 1UW

The Banking Ombudsman
70 Gray's Inn Road
London WC1X 8NB
0171-404 9944

The Building Societies Association
3 Savile Row
London W1X 1AF
0171-437 0655

The Building Societies Commission
15 Great Marlborough Street
London W1V 2LL
0171-437 9992

The Building Society Ombudsman
35-37 Grosvenor Gardens
London SW1X 7AW
0171-931 0044

Chartered Association of Certified Accountants
29 Lincoln's Inn Fields
London WC2A 3EE
0171-242 6855

Financial Intermediaries, Managers and Brokers Regulatory
   Association (Fimbra, now PIA)
Hertsmere House
Hertsmere Road
London E14 4AB
0171-538 8860

Institute of Actuaries
Staple Inn Hall
High Holborn
London WC1V 7QJ
0171-242 0106

Institute of Chartered Accountants in England and Wales
   (ICAEW)
PO Box 433
Chartered Accountants Hall
Moorgate Place
London EC2P 2BJ
0171-920 8100

Institute of Chartered Accountants in Ireland
Chartered Accountants House
87-89 Pembroke Road
Ballsbridge
Dublin 4
Ireland
010 353166 80400

Institute of Chartered Accountants in Scotland
27 Queen Street
Edinburgh EH2 1LA
0131-225 5673

Insurance Brokers' Registration Council (IBRC)
15 St Helen's Place
London EC3A 6DS
0171-588 4387

The Insurance Ombudsman Bureau
City Gate One
135 Park Street
London SE1 9EA
0171-928 4488

Investment Management Regulatory Organisation Ltd (IMRO)
Broadwalk House
6 Appold Street
London EC2A 2AA
0171-628 6022

Investors Compensation Scheme
Gavrelle House
2-14 Bunhill Row
London EC1Y 8RA
0171-638 1240

Law Society
113 Chancery Lane
London WC2A 1PL
0171-242 1222

Law Society of Northern Ireland
Law Society House
98 Victoria Street
Belfast BT1 3JZ
0232-231 614

Law Society of Scotland
The Law Society's Hall
26 Drumsheugh Gardens
Edinburgh EH3 7YR
0131-226 7411

Life Assurance and Unit Trust Regulator Organisation
    (Lautro, now PIA)
Centre Point
103 New Oxford Street
London WC1A 1QH
0171-379 0444

National Savings
Sales and Information Unit
Freepost BJ 881
Lytham St Anne's FYO 1YN

The Office of the Investment Ombudsman
6 Frederick's Place
London EC2R 8BT
0171-796 3065

Personal Investment Authority (PIA)
3/4 Royal Exchange Buildings

London EC3V 3NL
0171-929 0072

Personal Investment Authority Ombudsman
6th Floor
1 London Wall
London EC2Y 5EA
0171-600 3838

The ProShare Association
Freepost KE 8391
London EC2B 2LD
0171-971 0061

Securities and Futures Authority (SFA)
Cottons Centre
Cottons Lane
London SE1 2QB
0171-378 9000

Securities and Investments Board (SIB)
Gavrelle House
2-14 Bunhill Row
London EC1Y 8RA
0171-638 1240

Unit Trust Information Service
0181-207 1361

Sharedealing Made Simple – Phone Sharelink on 0121–200–2242.

THE 🛡 EXPRESS

THE EXPRESS Guides:

Your Money
How to Make the Most of it (Second Edition)
Niki Chesworth

◆ a practical, reliable guide aimed at cutting
through financial jargon
◆ invaluable advice on everything from
banking and taxes to retirement
◆ essential to make your money work for you

£7.99 Paperback 0 7494 1641 6
128 pages 1995

Be Your Own Boss!
How to Set Up a Successful Small Business
David McMullan

◆ lays out all the facts you need to know before
choosing and setting up your own business
◆ highlights common problems and potential
minefields in a new business

£7.99 Paperback 0 7494 1187 2
128 pages 1994

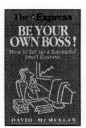

Great Ideas for Making Money
Niki Chesworth

◆ 70 inspiring ideas on making money from
antiques dealing to window cleaning
◆ advice on how to turn your ideas into profits

£7.99 Paperback 0 7494 1188 0
224 pages 1994

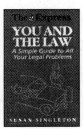

You And The Law
A Simple Guide to all Your Legal Problems
Susan Singleton

◆ a jargon free guide to remove the confusion
surrounding the legal system
◆ practical advice on everything from tax and
employment rights to divorce
◆ advice on how to deal with solicitors and
legal actions

£6.99 Paperback 0 7494 1133 0
120 pages 1994

**Available from all good book shops or to obtain further
information please contact the publishers at the address below:**

**Kogan Page Ltd
Pentonville Road, London N1 9JN
Tel: 0171 278 0433, Fax: 0171 837 6348**

Index

Index of Advertisers